T0198498

The Garland of Mahamudra Practices

The Garland of Mahamudra Practices

A Translation of Kunga Rinchen's *Clarifying the Jewel Rosary of the Profound Fivefold Path*

Translated and introduced by Khenchen Könchog Gyaltshen Rinpoche

Co-translated and edited by Katherine Rogers

Snow Lion
Boulder

Snow Lion
An imprint of Shambhala Publications, Inc.
4720 Walnut Street
Boulder, Colorado 80301
www.shambhala.com

The Tibetan title of Kun-dga'-rin-chen's text is *lNga ldan nor bu'i
'phreng ba'i gsal byed*

Printed in the United States of America

⊗This edition is printed on acid-free paper that meets the
American National Standards Institute Z39.48 Standard.
♻Shambhala Publications makes every effort to print on recycled
paper. For more information please visit www.shambhala.com.
Distributed in the United States by Penguin Random House LLC
and in Canada by Random House of Canada Ltd

The Library of Congress catalogues the previous edition of this title as follows:
Kun-dga'-rin-chen, 1475–1527
The Garland of Mahamudra practices.
Includes index.
ISBN 978-0-93793-835-5 (1st ed.)
ISBN 978-1-55939-173-3 (2nd ed.)
1. Mahāmudrā (Tantric rite). 2. Meditation (Tantric Buddhism).
3. Bka'-rgyud-pa (Sect)—Liturgy. I. Gyaltsen, Khenpo Rinpochay
Könchok, 1946–. II. Rogers, Katherine L. III. Title. IV. Title: Clarifying
the jewel rosary of the profound fivefold path.
BQ8921.M35K84 1986
294.3'443
86-22019

Contents

5

Foreword

The Fivefold Path of Mahamudra embodies the essence of Buddha's teachings — that vast ocean of sutras and tantras — on the actual practice of meditation. For those who are ready, it is a supreme method for attaining Buddhahood in one lifetime. This commentary, *Clarifying the Jewel Rosary of the Profound Fivefold Path,* was written in the sixteenth century by Gyalwang Kunga Rinchen,[1] the second Victorious One. It is translated into English for those fortunate beings who are interested, from the bottom of their hearts, in attaining liberation.

Kunga Rinchen's text begins with the most basic instructions and proceeds to the most advanced and profound. The student's first step — without which no other is possible — is to turn away from cyclic existence and toward enlightenment. The preparatory practices help one to take this step and, if they are earnestly followed, stabilize one in the new orientation by purifying one's nature. This brings the blessing of empowerment: the student's original wish to move toward enlightenment is gradually transformed into the ability to do so.

Striving to understand the condition of oneself and all other sentient beings, one develops love and compassion.

With these comes a determination to attain enlightenment — not for oneself, but so that one can better help all sentient beings. This deep, spontaneous cherishing of others is bodhichitta, the culmination of the preparatory practices.

Bodhichitta is also the first of the actual practices of the fivefold path, the other four being deity yoga, guru yoga, mahamudra, and dedication. The aspirant who practices all of them well is providing the causes for becoming a Buddha. For the beginner, Kunga Rinchen discusses these practices in sequence. For the advanced student, the five branches are a unified whole: each arises from and merges into all the others, and together they *are* the enlightened state.

This translation was made in the spirit of the oral tradition as a manual of practice for students at the meditation centers led by Khenpo Könchog Gyaltsen. The introduction and explanatory notes are based on his comments and answers to questions.

The translators are grateful to His Holiness, the Drikung Kyabgön Chetsang Rinpochay, for blessing them with the preface to this work. They are also grateful to Julia Rogers for editorial help, to Chris Achstetter for editing the life story of Kunga Rinchen, to Chris Achstetter and Richard Rogers for proofreading and indexing, and to Stephen Willing, who read the manuscript and made many helpful suggestions.

By the power of the merit of this work, may the problems of the world — sickness, famine, and conflict — be alleviated; may sentient beings quickly be liberated from all suffering and attain the state of Vajradhara, composite of the Four Buddha Bodies.

Khenpo Könchog Gyaltsen
Katherine Rogers
Washington, D.C., 1986

Preface

The excellent teacher, Buddha, with great skill and compassion, turned the three wheels of doctrine[2] in order to guide all sentient beings to the stages of liberation and omniscience. His teachings — the sutras and tantras — are as vast as the ocean, and they have been commented on by many scholars and realized beings in India and Tibet.

One of the great scholars of Tibet was Lord Jigten Sumgön (1143-1217),[3] known as the second Nāgārjuna. Expanding on the essence of the Buddha's teaching concerning the true nature (or natural mode of being) of reality, he turned many wheels of doctrine for his hundreds of thousands of disciples. Later, his teachings were compiled by one of his disciples, the greatly realized scholar Chennga Drikung Lingpa. This compilation, entitled *The One Thought: The Supreme Teaching of All Buddhas,* but often referred to as '*Gong Chik*' (*One Thought*), contains the very essence of the sutras and tantras.

Many scholars have commented on this great compilation, *Gong Chik.* Important commentaries were written by Jigten Sumgön's disciples: several by Chen-nga Drikung Lingpa himself; a great commentary by Dorje Sherap entitled *Dorshema; Gargonma* by Gartamba Chodingpa; and

Rinchangma by Tupba Rinchen Changchup.

Other important commentaries were written later: *The Clarification*, by Shamar Shipa, the fourth Shamarpa Rinpochay; the great commentary by Karmapa Mikyö Dorje; *Questions and Answers on the Difficult Points of Gong Chik*, by Gyalwang Kunga Rinchen (one of the great reincarnations of Lord Jigten Sumgön); *Commentary on Gong Chik: the Light of the Sun* and *The Lamp Clearing Away the Darkness of the Difficult Points*, by Künkyen Chökyi Trakpa; and many more.

From another point of view — that of the actual practice of meditation — Lord Gampopa (1079-1153) drew together all of the teachings of the Buddha into one fivefold system. To this system his lineage holder and main disciple, Pakdru Dorje Gyalpo (1110-1170), later gave the name "the profound fivefold path of mahamudra."

Pakdru Dorje Gyalpo himself established many students on the paths of fruition and liberation and wrote *Verses on the Fivefold Path*, as well as other works. Pakdru Dorje Gyalpo's chief disciple and successor was Lord Jigten Sumgön. He placed a great emphasis on his teacher's works and himself wrote *The Grey Wings of the Fivefold Path*, *Setting an Example of the Fivefold Path*, and others.

Texts concerning the fivefold profound path have been written by teachers of the Trobu Kagyu and Taklung Kagyu lineages; and a teacher in the Drukpa Kagyu lineage, Gyalwa Yang Gönpa, wrote about it in his *Drop of Nectar: the Fivefold Path*. Other commentaries are by Situ Chökyi Jung-ne, and there are teachings on this path by Drukpa Künkyen Pema Karbo in *The Kernel of Mind*. Many other works on this profound path were written by lamas before and after these. Nowadays the students who seek liberation generally follow the practices as set forth in the work called the *The Teachings of Dharmakīrti*, by Dharmakīrti, a great teacher of the Drikung Kagyu lineage.

Gyalwang Kunga Rinchen, who wrote *Questions and Answers on the Difficult Points of Gong Chik*, also wrote

Clarifying the Jewel Rosary of the Profound Fivefold Path.
This has been translated into English by the Kagyu Abbot
Könchog Gyaltsen and Katherine Rogers, for the inspira-
tion of those who are engaged in hearing, thinking about,
and meditating on the teachings of the Buddha.

The particular value of this work is that Gyalwang Kunga
Rinchen presents the pure teaching of Jigten Sumgön and
Pakdru Dorje Gyalpo, without any additions or embellish-
ments of his own. It is strictly based on the teachings of the
Buddha, and it is clear and easy to understand. Although
many commentaries were written between the time of Jigten Sumgön and Kunga Rinchen, Kunga Rinchen analysed
them all carefully before composing his work.

May the virtue of translating and publishing this work
give strength to the spreading of the precious teachings of
the Buddha. The beings who meet with this profound path,
which has marvelous blessings, are fortunate; having
attained this blessing, they will quickly arrive at the rank of
Supreme Buddhahood.

This preface was written on the fifth day of the tenth
month of the wood-mouse year, November 27, 1984, by
His Holiness, Könchog Tenzin Kunsang Trinley Lhün-
dup, the Drikung Kyabgön Chetsang Rinpochay, the successor of Drikung Kagyu Lord Jigten Sumgön.

Introduction: The Fivefold Path

What is mahamudra? It is the Buddha nature, the basic mind within all sentient beings. To know it is to know the true nature of all phenomena, and to actualize it is to become a Buddha, to be one with all the Buddha qualities. The Buddha nature, mahamudra, is there always, but for those whose attention is turned away from it, it remains a secret. To discover it, to uncover it, requires practice and the guidance of a truly spiritual teacher.

The *preparatory practices* of the fivefold path develop the reorientation, purification, and strength required for the practice of mahamudra. The *actual practices* are the path itself, which leads to enlightenment.

The *general preparatory practices* are four: refuge, which saves us from mistaken paths; Vajrasattva, which removes obstacles to the path; mandala offering, which brings meritorious power; and guru devotion, which brings blessings that empower us to pursue the path.

Refuge is the most important preparatory practice, because without it one will not seriously undertake the others. To take refuge is to orient oneself firmly on the path to Buddhahood and turn away from cyclic existence. To do this, one must really understand that cyclic existence —

14

samsara — is unavoidably a state of confusion and suffering; then one will consider how to free oneself from it.

We ourselves do not know how. Generally, we are absorbed in trying to be comfortable in samsara, because we know it and are attached to its pleasant experiences. When we decide to reorient ourselves, we have to rely on instructions from one who has done it, who has already traveled the path to enlightenment. Thus we go for refuge to the Three Jewels: the Buddha, the teacher; the dharma, his teachings; and the sangha, the spiritual community.

Turning away from samsara does not mean just studying the dharma and considering enlightenment; one can know the dharma intellectually and not have deep understanding. Understanding comes through the four "ordinary foundations": meditation on impermanence, on cause and effect, on the troubles of samsara, and on the preciousness and rarity of human life. Being in a human body now, we can start on the path to Buddhahood; this is an opportunity to be seized.

These foundations are called the four ways of turning the mind, turning it away from samsara. Without these meditations, one's refuge is incomplete. One needs to clearly understand the nature of samsara and then firmly orient oneself toward enlightenment; in this way one draws near the path.

In order to attain enlightenment, one needs to accumulate wisdom and compassion, the two collections; when they are complete, one will be able to actualize the four bodies of a Buddha. Developing wisdom and compassion is not a small task — it demands a great deal of strength. And this strength is acquired through the preliminary practices: Vajrasattva, mandala offering, and guru yoga. These bring purification, strengthening, and special empowering blessings.

Vajrasattva practice clears away obstacles on the path. The basic mind is like a mirror, which cannot reflect objects when it is dusty; when it is nicely cleaned, it can reflect any object clearly. The basic mind of any sentient being is the Buddha nature, but it is covered with the dust of samsara. Vajrasattva meditation is a powerful purification practice.

Mandala offering is a way of developing and sustaining wisdom (the realization of mahamudra) and compassion (the profound bodhichitta). Feeling deeply the wish that oneself and all sentient beings may attain enlightenment, we offer the mandala — which represents the entire universe — to the enlightened ones, full of compassion and wisdom. We give it all away, ourselves and everything. This offering helps us cut our clinging and attachment to this life. In addition, the merit one acquires through mandala offering gives one the strength to nurture the mind of bodhichitta.

Guru yoga bestows blessings. The teacher is the example, the model. If we see the teacher as ordinary, our minds will remain in the ordinary state, but if we see him or her as Vajradhara, we will lift the state of our minds. Viewing one's teacher as Vajradhara is a way of uniting one's mind with the Vajradhara state. Through thinking of the teacher as Vajradhara, we receive the blessings empowering us to achieve that state ourselves. When we view the teacher as compassionate and wise, the power of our devotion eliminates the hesitations in our minds; this we call the guru's blessing. The teacher must indeed have good qualities and realizations; but the important energy in guru yoga is that of the practitioner — the student's admiration and gratitude.

When you really study and practice, some little bit of experience dawns in your mind, and with it an inexpressible confidence and joy. When this occurs, you feel a true nonartificial devotion. This is devotion not merely from faith in the teacher but from one's own experience, and it is the experience of true guru yoga. Within this deep devotion one receives the four empowerments, which carry the special blessings enabling one to develop the four Buddha Bodies.

The *special preparatory practices* are the cultivation of love
and compassion, a very gentle mind wishing that all sentient beings may have happiness and be free from suffering.
Developing these two is necessary, but that alone is not
sufficient. What must one do to bring happiness to sentient
beings? An ignorant person cannot help. So we must become wise, must reach enlightenment. Toward that end we
need to follow a perfect path; and the path of mahamudra is
such a path.

We begin by cultivating a strong mind wishing to achieve
enlightenment for the sake of others; that mind is *bodhichitta*. Without it, all practices are futile; with it, the eventual
attainment of enlightenment is certain. The only way to
develop love, compassion, and bodhichitta is through deep
concern for other sentient beings; if they did not exist, love
would remain a mystery. Thus, it is clear that one's own
enlightenment depends on other sentient beings: without
them to cherish, one can make no progress on the path.

Bodhichitta, the last of the preparatory practices, is at the
same time the first of the *five actual practices:* bodhichitta,
yidam practice, guru yoga, mahamudra, and dedication.

Through *yidam practice* (deity yoga) one actualizes all the
qualities of the Buddha in oneself. The Buddha nature —
the essence of all sentient beings — is said to be really a
secret. Teaching about that secret is given by the Buddha:
in meditation one becomes one with the yidam deity, in
order to recognize the deity nature in oneself. That is the
secret of tantra and why yidam practice is called the essence
of secret mantra. You are transforming your ordinary state
into the pure state, visualizing yourself and all sentient
beings — the whole universe — as transformed into Buddhas in a Buddha field.

Guru yoga is called the essence of knowledge, the knowledge that brings one to enlightenment; that knowledge is
received from the teacher. This yoga has two levels. The
preparatory practice of guru yoga is the cultivation of devotion by viewing one's teacher as Vajradhara. In the actual

practice of mahamudra, guru yoga is the establishing in one's own continuum of the causes for actualizing the four bodies of a Buddha.

Mahamudra is beyond thought and even further beyond words — inconceivable and inexpressible. It is enlightenment, the pure basic mind, the essence of meaning, the true nature, emptiness; all of these phrases are attempts to point to a moon which the student cannot yet see. Those who have realized mahamudra know that it can be done; and, to suggest what that realization means, they speak of the unity of emptiness and appearance, of pure form and emptiness, of the relative and the absolute.

Realizing this unity is realizing mahamudra, but describing it imposes the duality of thought. The teachers speak of setting one's mind in emptiness, in nonduality; they cannot impart their experience of this, but they can guide the student's meditative practice toward that experience. Emptiness is the luminous nature of the mind — not its usual busyness with thinking. For a beginner, 'without thought' just means an empty head, but that is not what is meant. This luminous nature of the mind is something beyond duality and nonduality.

For beginners, the teacher points out mahamudra, the view of emptiness, through the Madhyamika reasonings based on the teachings of Nāgārjuna. The students will understand on the basis of instruction, but they will not yet know. They must practice, must work, to reveal the Buddha nature in themselves.

Kunga Rinchen makes it clear that samsara and mahamudra are one; generally we think they are two things, one terrible and the other wonderful. Being still not enlightened, the student feels that enlightenment is different and far away; but actually the basis and the goal are one. Cyclic existence is not something separate from enlightenment, is not separate from the Buddha nature.

We think we are grounded in samsara and need to get somewhere else, but that is a misunderstanding. Thinking that we have to discover emptiness to counteract the afflictions, we set up a polarity, an opposition, between them. But if we do that, we can fall into the mistake of merely refusing to think about afflictions and thinking instead about emptiness. That is not what is sought. One needs to realize that all phenomena — afflictions, too — have the nature of emptiness; they are not separate from emptiness.

Mahamudra is just things as they are, the true nature of phenomena. When the teacher points to mahamudra, he or she is showing what the Buddha taught; what the Buddha taught is just that. To say that fire is hot is not to accept or reject it — when heat has been experienced, it is understood. Mahamudra is similarly just the way things are; experiencing it is beyond any assertion.

Dedication is the beginning and the end of practice; our study and work are not for ourselves. The root of virtue within us, the Buddha nature, is like a drop of water: alone, it will dry up and vanish, but if we cast it into the ocean it will never dry. So if we dedicate our drop of virtue to the ocean of wisdom, it will add to the ocean forever, helping all sentient beings to achieve enlightenment.

Clarifying the Jewel Rosary of the Profound Fivefold Path

by Kunga Rinchen

Introduction

Namo guru. Homage to the guru.[4] I bow down respectfully to you, the lord who is the Fourth Body, the entity of the great Vajradhara, the pervading lord, composite in one of the Three Bodies.[5]

The Truth Body is that which is — from the beginning — profound, clear emptiness, unproduced and without inherent existence.

The Victorious Complete Enjoyment Body, possessing the nine graceful states, is the union of emptiness and compassion, utterly pure, untouched by the faults of dualistic thought.

The manifold Emanation Body brings about the fruition and liberation of sentient beings in all realms, using all the Buddha lineages, taking whatever forms will be helpful to sentient beings.

21

The four genuine validities[6] are: the teachings of the Conqueror, the commentaries, the realizations of yogis, and dependent-arising. The essence of the Buddha's teaching can be shown by the delineation of these four validities.

First, the fivefold path will be explained and made flawlessly clear, like the Buddha's teaching. As the Lord Jigten Sumgön lists them, "The five aspects of this path are bodhichitta, the yidam deity, the teacher, mahamudra, and dedication." This teaching is given many names: the diamond verses of the fivefold path; the song of realization of the fivefold path; the secret speech of the fivefold path; the grey wings of the fivefold path; and setting an example of the fivefold path. In *The Essence of the Teachings of the Mahayana Vehicle,* the great spiritual friend, the scholar Drukyamo, called this path "the ultimate pure Sugata teaching."

Drukyamo also wrote:

> One must think in solitude on the teachings obtained through the kindness of the lama; one must cultivate the four practices — the very life of the path, which prevents the teachings from degenerating; and one must cultivate the five meditations, the fruit. Together, these encompass the complete meaning of the teachings of the Buddha.

This injunction arises from the valid teachings of the Conqueror. It is said that the three streams of lineage[7] are combined together; this means that within the three wheels of teachings of the Buddha, the wholly perfect teacher, is the wheel of definitive meaning and that from this wheel is extracted the essence — ten sutras.

In the *Uttaratantra of the Great Vehicle,* the seven vajra topics[8] are explained:

> From the Buddha comes the doctrine;
> From the doctrine comes the assembly of Superiors;
> From the assembly, the essential wisdom element is attained.

Attainment of that wisdom is attainment of the
ultimate enlightened state.

This is the meaning of the fivefold path: One must receive the quintessential instructions from the teacher. One
must think in solitude about those instructions. Then one
must proceed to the four contemplations, the four practices, and the five meditations.[9]

Again, Drukyamo says in his *Auto-Commentary:*

As the rays of the sun penetrate the mist, cut
through the external superimpositions by means of
the four knowledges. By means of the four contemplations, clear away the faults of the vessel (the
mind) until it is as pure as ambrosia. By means of
the four practices, which are like alchemy in their
power to transform, fulfill the purpose of the
teaching. By means of the five meditations, which
are for the purpose of attaining the fruit, gather up
the meaning of the teaching.

THE FOUR KNOWLEDGES

These four are to be known: the root of the path, attending
to the lama; how to pay attention to the lama; how to please
the lama; hearing the words of the lama, thinking about
them, and meditating on them.

THE FOUR CONTEMPLATIONS

These are to be contemplated[10]: the antidote to attachment
to this life — contemplation of impermanence; the antidote
to ill-directed activity and to laziness — contemplation of
the rarity of attaining leisure and fortune; the antidote to
attachment to the pleasures of existence — contemplation
of the faults of cyclic existence; and, as a way of attaining a
meaningful life — contemplation of the benefits of liberation.

THE FOUR PRACTICES

These four are to be practiced: the practice of refuge, through taking refuge; the practice of individual liberation; the practice of bodhichitta; and the practice of Secret Mantra.

THE FIVE MEDITATIONS

These are the five meditations: cultivation of the main causes of Buddhahood — love, compassion, and bodhichitta; meditation on the yidam diety, the essence of Secret Mantra; meditation on the teacher, the essence of good qualities; meditation on mahamudra, the essence of the meaning; and performing the dedication, the essence of the fruit.

Holding to the quintessential instructions regarding the above knowledges, contemplations, practices, and meditations, one engages in the preparatory practices, then the actual practices, and then the concluding practices.

PREPARATORY PRACTICES
Common Preparatory Practices
Special Preparatory Practices

Common Preparatory Practices

These fall into four parts: (1) teachings on refuge in the Three Jewels, which save one from mistaken paths;[11] (2) teachings regarding meditation on Vajrasattva and repetition of the 100-syllable mantra, which clear away obstacles on the path;[12] (3) teachings concerning the mandala, which completes the collections[13] of the path; and (4) teachings on the actual practice of guru yoga, which brings the bestowal of blessings.[14]

I. REFUGE

First, sitting comfortably in the sevenfold posture of concentration,[15] you are to meditate on the impermanence of all created things. Meditate in accordance with these words of Buddha:

> Who knows whether one will die tomorrow?
> From now on, make effort at practice.
> The lord of death — great fear —
> Is not your friend.

Contemplating the Rarity of Attaining Leisure and Fortune
The Master Shāntideva said:

27

A precious human body, as well as leisure and fortune, are all very hard to find. These fruitions of temporary and definite goodness[16] can be attained. If one does not make use of the leisure and fortune of this life, then how can good opportunities arise in the future?

One must meditate on this.

Contemplating the Faults of Cyclic Existence

One must meditate on cyclic existence as without essence, in accordance with these words of the Buddha:

> Hell beings are tortured by fire,
> Hungry ghosts by hunger and thirst;
> Animals are tortured by eating one another,
> Human beings by dissatisfaction;
> Gods are tortured by nonawareness,
> Demigods by fighting and quarreling.
> In cyclic existence there is no absolute happiness —
> Not a drop, not so much as the point of a needle.

Contemplating the Benefits of Liberation

The Lord Nāgārjuna said:

> Three aspects of body,
> Four aspects of speech,
> Three aspects of mind;[17]
> These are the path:
> Not drinking alcohol, earning a living rightly,
> Harming no-one, giving gifts respectfully,
> Honoring the deserving, and treating all with loving
>   kidness.
> Practicing these will free you from unhappy states
>   and bring happy ones.
> If you have practiced well the systems of people,
> Then it is no great distance to the realm of gods.
> If you climb the stairs of gods and humanity, you
>   draw near to liberation.

One meditates on the 16 virtues. One generates a wish to attain to the benefits of liberation. One generates a fear of the faults of cyclic existence. To attain liberation from the suffering of cyclic existence and to attain the benefits of liberation, one must generate a mind going for refuge to the Three Jewels.

The Dharma Lord Jigten Sumgön said, "One must go for refuge by means of three special features — those of refuge, of mind, and of time." The special feature of refuge includes the teacher, the yidam deity, the Three Jewels, and the Dakas, Dakinis, and Dharma Protectors. The special feature of mind is to generate a mind beneficial to all sentient beings. The special feature of time is that one is going for refuge from now until the attainment of enlightenment.

Visualize in the space in front of you the objects of refuge on an excellent throne.[18] Make the seven branches of offering.[19] The verbal expression of this is:

> May the lama lead all sentient beings throughout space, oneself and others — all the kind mothers — to liberation. May the yidam deity bestow blessings on our minds. May the Buddhas give teachings. May the dharma become the path. May the members of the sangha become our friends. May the Dakas and Dakinis achieve attainments. May the Dharma Protectors subdue obstacles.

Repeat these words and think about them. Then go for refuge, thinking:

> From this time until I attain the essence of
>   enlightenment,
> I go for refuge to the glorious root and lineage
>   lamas, embodiments of wisdom, compassion, and
>   power.
> I go for refuge to the assembly of yidam deities.
> I go for refuge to the exalted Buddhas in the ten
>   directions.[20]

I go for refuge to the excellent teaching in the ten
   directions.
I go for refuge to the superior sangha in the ten
   directions.
I go for refuge to the Dakas, Dakinis, and Dharma
   Protectors, who have eyes of wisdom and feet of
   miraculous power.

Go for refuge, thinking of the good qualities of the objects
of refuge. Pray for the attainment of your aims, thinking:

May the meaning of impermanence be generated in
my mind. May negative conditions become posi-
tive. May I be liberated through realization. May
compassion ripen others' minds. Please bestow
blessings on me that my devotion to the teacher may
be stable and that I may keep my promise. Please
bestow blessings on me that I may become skilled in
the method of dependent-arising. Please bestow
blessings on me that whatever relationships I may
enter into may have meaning. Please bestow blessings on me that I may generate in my mind the
meditative stabilization of the stages of generation
and completion.[21] Please cause the generation of
supreme realization in my mind.

Then, cause the objects of refuge to dissolve into yourself.
Set your mind in the tranquility of the mahamudra state.[22]
   Then, generate a mind thinking:

May all sentient beings attain Buddhahood. In
order to establish them all in Buddhahood, I will
practice the recitation and meditation of Vajrasattva.

II. VAJRASATTVA MEDITATION

Visualize at the crown of your head a lotus flower, on which
there is a full-moon disc; in the center of the disc is a blue
vajra, in which there is a syllable *hūṃ*.[23]   The syllable *hūṃ*

is then completely transformed into Vajrasattva, whose body is the white color of the reflecction of sunlight shining on the peak of a snow mountain. Vajrasattva is in the half-lotus posture, with the toe of his right foot on the crown of your head. His right hand, at his heart, holds a vajra; his left hand, at his waist, holds a bell. He is adorned with various precious ornaments. The *hūṃ* syllable is in the center of the moon at the heart of Vajrasattva, and around it is the 100-syllable mantra. From the *hūṃ*, light radiates and pervades all of space. This light removes the obstructions[24] of all sentient beings and then spreads to the Buddha fields in the form of offerings.

Then draw into your own heart, from the heart of the Buddhas and Bodhisattvas, a stream of ambrosia, which is wisdom and compassion. The stream descends from them to Vajrasattva and through his body; it then flows from his right toe into your body through the crown of your head. You are then cleansed of the collections of faults, wrong-doings, and obstructions, accumulated beginninglessly. The stream of ambrosia fills your whole body from your feet upward.

Then meditate that your body becomes transformed into the body of Vajrasattva. Observe the 100-syllable mantra that surrounds the *hūṃ* at the heart of Vajrasattva, still seated at the crown of your head. Then repeat the 100-syllable mantra:[25]

Oṃ vazra satvasamaya manupalaya vazrasatvatenopa tishtadidhomebhawa sutokhyomebhawa supokhyo-mebhawa anuraktomebhawa sarva siddhim me-prayatsa sarvakarma sutsame tsittan shriyakuruhung ha ha ha ha ho bhagawan sarvatathagata vazramame muntsa vazribhawa mahasamayasatva āḥ:

OM Vajrasattva, please bestow blessings on me. May you be pleased with me; may you be steadily pleased. May you bestow on me all of the actual accomplishments.[26] May my mind be established

firmly in all activities. *Hūṃ ha ha ha ha hoḥ* all the
blessed Tathāgatas, may I be liberated fully in the
vajra. Please grant me the actual vajra mind, great
pledge being, *āḥ hūṃ*.

Then think:

Through ignorance, I fall away from and contradict
my pledges. Please protect me, Lord of Teachers.
You are the chief holder of the vajra. You are the
embodiment of compassion. Leader of sentient
beings, please protect me.

Think that the Blessed One then says: "You are freed of
obstructions." You should think that Vajrasattva, having
accepted your prayers, then dissolves into you. You should
then set your mind on the meaning of Vajrasattva, the
union of appearance and emptiness.

III. THE MANDALA, FOR THE COMPLETION OF THE COLLECTIONS

This section has two parts, mandala establishment and
mandala offering.

Mandala Establishment

If possible, make the mandala of precious jewels. If that is
not possible, then make it out of clay, wood, or stone. If
precious jewels are used, the mandala should be at least four
inches high. If other materials are used, it cannot be less
than one foot. Whatever the mandala is made of, its substance and shape must be perfect. Why? In order that one
may be born in a pure realm.

Hold the mandala in your left hand. Holding an
ornament[27] in your right hand, clean the mandala with your
right arm. Think that just as the mandala is free from dust,
so is your mind free of karma, afflictive obstructions, and
obstructions to omniscience.

In the center of the mandala place a pile of rice. Then

visualize that on a cushion of perfect shape[28] is the form of the lama, which is the embodiment of all the Buddhas in the shape of the teacher, Vajradhara, surrounded by the assembled lineage lords. In front of Vajradhara on a perfect cushion are the assembled yidam deities. On a seat to the right of Vajradhara is the Buddha. To the left of Vajradhara are the sangha and the great Bodhisattvas. Behind him are the precious teachings. In between are the Dakas, Dakinis, and Dharma Protectors.

In the *Samādhirāja Sutra*, it is written:

> The one who, whether going or staying,
> Remembers the king of supreme sages —
> That one the Buddhas will stay with forever.
> Such a one will attain Buddhahood.

You must meditate as though all these assembled beings were actually present.

Mandala Offering

If there is a second mandala, place it on the altar. If there is not, then begin by observing the beings assembled before you. Then, clean the mandala well. In the center, place Mount Meru; in the east, Videha; in the south, Jambudvipa (our world); in the west, Godānīya; in the north, Kuru. To the left of Mount Meru place the sun; and to the right, the moon. In the center of Mount Meru, all the wealth of gods and human beings is piled up. Then say:

> The ground is scented with incense and strewn with flowers. It is adorned with Mount Meru, the four continents, the sun and moon. Thinking of this as a Buddha field, I offer it. May all sentient beings enjoy the pure realms.
>
> *Guru idaṃ ratna maṇḍalakaṃ niryātayāmi.* To you, the Guru Yidam, I offer, with this mandala, my body, resources, and roots of virtue.[29] Accepting these through your compassion, please enable me to generate the supreme realization.

> To you, the Three Jewels, I offer, with this mandala, my body, resources, and roots of virtue; accepting these, please enable me to generate the supreme realization.
>
> To you, the Dakas and Dakinis, I offer, with this mandala, my body, resources and roots of virtue; accepting these, please enable me to generate the supreme realization.

Make this prayer petition many times. This mandala is very important for completing the accumulations of compassion and wisdom. The Buddha said:

> Until you complete the roots of virtue,
> You will not attain the ultimate (meaning of) emptiness.

Then, having caused the assembly to dissolve into yourself, set your mind on the meaning of profound nonduality.

IV. GURU YOGA

There is one way of cultivating guru yoga, called "in the manner of the lord of lineage," in which the lama is at the crown of one's head. But, here, in this practice of guru yoga, the lama is visualized in front of oneself. When receiving the four empowerments, visualize the following:

In the space in front of you, there is a precious throne held up by eight lions; the throne is broad and vast. On it is the syllable *paṃ*, from which arises a lotus. On the lotus is the letter *āḥ*, which becomes a moon. On the moon is the syllable *raṃ*, which turns into the sun. On the sun-seat is your own root lama, having the nature of kindness, in the form of Vajradhara, with a blue body, one face, and two hands. In his right hand is a five-spoke vajra; in his left is a bell, with a five-spoke vajra handle. The vajra and bell are crossed at his heart. His hair is bound up in a knot at the top of his head, and he is wearing a crown of bone and precious jewels, earrings, and three necklaces — one short, one to his chest, one to his navel. He is also wearing a belt, a bracelet, ankle ornaments, and precious garments of silk. He is endowed with the 32 major marks and the 80 minor marks of a Buddha.

Vajradhara is sitting in the vajra posture; over his head are the lineage lamas, one above the other in a line of succession reaching eventually to the actual Vajradhara. Direct your thoughts to the visualized Vajradhara, thinking:

> To the Glorious Lama, the embodiment of the Four Buddha Bodies, I offer all possible things; I offer my body, speech, and mind, as well as the three offerings, outer, inner, and secret.[30] The object offered, the offerer, and the act of offering — these three are of one nature. I offer these, free from elaboration, as one great equal taste. Please grant me the actual accomplishment[31] effortlessly. I offer, without expectation, the outer, inner, and secret offerings, as well as my own body, resources, and collections of virtue.

Say the following prayer-mantra as many times as possible:

> I pray to the Glorious Lama, master of the four Buddhas' bodies, crown-jewel of the entire Dakpo Kagyu lineage, leader of sentient beings, teacher of the ultimate path, lord of compassion, regent of the Buddha, of peerless kindness, incomparable teacher. Vajradhara, heed my prayer, Great Drikungpa! I pray to you. Look upon me with compassion! Empower me with the blessings! The two attainments—bestow them now! Spontaneously establish the two benefits![32] Here bestow the fruit!

While reciting in this way, visualize that the actual Vajradhara dissolves into the lama below him; each lineage lord dissolves into the one below, until all have dissolved into your root lama. Then receive the four empowerments,³³ while continuing to repeat the prayer-mantra.

The Four Empowerments

1. The First Empowerment

Visualize the Glorious Lama, Vajradhara, the embodiment of all good qualities, entering the opening in the center of the crown of your head and pray, "Please purify the tendencies of my waking state through the water of the vase empowerment. May my waking states be purified."

Through this supplication, white light radiates from the forehead of the lama and dissolves into your forehead, purifying you of the obstructions of the waking state. You obtain the vase empowerment, as well as the Emanation Body of the form-vajra manifestation.

2. The Second Empowerment

The Complete Enjoyment Body possesses vajra speech and thus can speak in the language of all sentient beings. Visualize the Complete Enjoyment Body entering the center of speech at your throat and think: "May the fuel of dreams be burned by the fire of the secret empowerment of supreme joy."

By the power of this prayer, red light radiates from the throat of the precious lama and dissolves into your throat, purifying you of the obstructions of the dream state. You obtain the secret empowerment as well as the Complete Enjoyment Body, which is vajra speech.

3. The Third Empowerment

Visualize the guru, nonconceptual *Dharmakāya* (the Truth Body), entering the center of your mind at your heart and think: "May the deep darkness of sleep be awakened by exalted wisdom." By the power of this prayer, blue light radiates from the heart of the precious lama and dissolves into your heart, purifying you of the obstructions of the deep sleep state. You obtain the empowerment of exalted wisdom and the Truth Body, which is vajra mind.

4. The Fourth Empowerment

Visualize the lord of sentient beings, the Innate Body (*Sahajakāya*), entering the center of the wisdom consciousness at your navel and think: "May I attain the unchanging joy through the bestowal of this great wisdom empowerment."

By the power of this prayer, yellow light radiates from the navel of the precious lama and dissolves into your navel, purifying you of the obstructions of the state of changing. You obtain the fourth empowerment and the Innate Body, which is the wisdom vajra. Then think:

> May the body, speech, mind, and wisdom of myself
> and all sentient beings throughout space become
> equal to your fourfold vajra state.[34] Please enable
> me to attain the supreme joy.

By the power of this prayer, the precious lama melts into a ray of light and dissolves into you. Think that the guru's body, speech, and mind and your own body, speech, and mind can no longer be differentiated. Then, set your mind in nonduality.

The esteemed Gampopa said:

> We are of the blessing lineage;[35]
> If the lama's blessing is not received,
> There is no way to realize the meaning of
> mahamudra.
> But for those who have the lama's blessing,
> That realization is not difficult.

In order to practice guru yoga, your mind must be very strong and steady. If, when you are practicing it, there is a limitation to your devotion, it will not work. To practice true guru yoga, you must think — from the very depths of your heart — of the kindness of the root and lineage gurus and of their good qualities of body, speech, and mind. So intense is this devotion that the hairs on your body will rise, tears will well into your eyes, and your voice will break. You have only the lama in your mind; your mind is attracted to the lama; you then wish to pray day and night to the lama. Until such blazing experiences of true guru yoga arise, you must make effort.

Special Preparatory Practices

These practices are for the cultivation of love, of compassion, and of bodhichitta.[36] In *The Song of Realization of the Fivefold Path*, the Precious Lord Jigten Sumgön said:

> If we race the steed of love and compassion
> For the benefit of ourselves and not for others,
> We will not receive the acclaim of gods and human
>   beings.
> Attend, therefore, to the preliminary steps.

I. LOVE

The cultivation of love (loving kindness) can be considered from several points of view: how it is generated; its true entity or nature; the increase of love; the activities of love; the error of neglecting to cultivate love; and the benefits of cultivating love — the fruits to be attained.

Generating Love

The ways of generating love are to understand the kindness of others and to repay their kindness. One should consider the kindness of the parents who have made possible this life, with this body and mind; one should consider the abbot and teacher who establish the pure rules of ethics and the teacher who indicates clearly what is to be adopted and what discarded. One should consider especially the great kindness of one's mother. Why? Because mothers give food without limit, in amounts as great as Mount Meru; they clothe their children well, as if in a cloud; the milk they give is as boundless as the ocean. Such thinking is the way to cultivate love.

The Entity or True Nature of Love

It is said, "When one sees a greatly beloved child, love is generated; when one comes in front of a leper, compassion is generated; when one meets with a friend, joy is generated. During sleep, equanimity is generated." Love itself arises, and by its own force gives one a desire to never be separated from the object of one's love.

The Increase of Love

The increase of love involves two practices: meditation on one's own mother and meditation extended to all sentient beings. When meditating on your own mother, remember her kindness and think, "May she have happiness."

This is not so much meditation as habituation or familiarization. Practice constantly in this way. Through the power of such familiarization, the entity of love will dawn.

Then, to increase that love, think that all sentient beings have been your mother and father and have been very kind. In a sutra it is said: "Nowhere in all of space is there a sentient being who has not been my parent." Meditate on all sentient beings just as you meditated on your own mother.

Meditating on all sentient beings in this way, you will generate love. If love is not generated, meditate again on your own mother; again generate love for your mother and then, in order to increase it, direct it toward all sentient beings, in all directions — east, south, west, and north.

The Activities of Love
Love and compassion clear away all conditions contrary to virtue. The evil Mara said to Buddha, "You are victorious, not by swords, wheels, or spears, but by the weapons of love and compassion." The activities of love give rise to good fortune and happiness, as illustrated by the life of King Champetop.[37]

The Error of Neglecting to Cultivate Love
Milarepa said:

> If one does not cultivate love and compassion, one falls to the lower vehicle.[38] Make effort at the practice of bodhichitta based on love and compassion.

The Benefits of Cultivating Love
Nāgārjuna says of those who practice love:

> Even though not liberated from cyclic existence,
> They attain the eight qualities of love;
> They receive the love of gods and human beings;
> They are protected; their minds are happy;
> They are not harmed by poison or weapons;
> They achieve their purposes effortlessly,
> And they are reborn in the realm of Brahmā.

II. COMPASSION

The Object of Observation of Compassion
For the generation of compassion, as for the generation of love, the object of observation is the mother. The wish to free all mothers from suffering is the very essence of compassion. Atīsha says in his *Treatise on Great Beings:*

> Those who, because of the wisdom they have realized, wish to relieve the suffering of others completely — those are great beings.

The power of compassion stirs in our hearts the wish to relieve the suffering of all sentient beings, just as we wish to free ourselves from suffering.

The Increase of Compassion

It is difficult to feel compassion toward someone who has done us harm. If we wish to harm such a person in return, we cannot feel compassion. To increase compassion, we should alternate our meditation, generating compassion first toward a friend and then toward an enemy, until the mind is purified and compassion is perfected.

The Activities of Compassion

The *Pundarika Karuna Sutra* says:

> There is one quality of Bodhisattvas that brings to the one who possesses it all the qualities of Bodhisattvas. What is that one quality? It is great compassion.

The Fruit To Be Attained

The Lord Phagmo Drupa said:

> When the stream of love flows steadily,
> The root of compassion is moistened.
> When the tree of bodhichitta is fully grown,
> The fruit of realization ripens
> And the flower of the tenth ground[39] blossoms.
> May the two purposes be achieved.

The cultivation of love and compassion enables one to attain the two conditions of high status (of gods and human beings) but not the condition of definite goodness (liberation).

III. BODHICHITTA

Lord Gampopa said, "High status in cyclic existence is temporary happiness; definite goodness is liberation." Even one who has attained the state of god or human being is not yet free from cyclic existence. Such a one must still cultivate bodhichitta. The great teacher Shāntideva said:

Bodhichitta is to be understood as two aspects:
The aspirational mind of enlightenment
And the actual mind of enlightenment.
Just as everyone knows the difference
Between wishing to go somewhere and actually
 going,
So the skillful know the differences between those
 two.

The two aspects are the mind striving toward enlightenment and the mind that has attained it.

Aspirational Bodhichitta
To cultivate the aspirational mind of enlightenment, make a
promise to attain the fruit. Do this by thinking:

I will set free those who are engulfed by the great
ocean of suffering of the three lower realms;[40] I will
set free all sentient beings, the mothers whose number is as limitless as the sky; and especially I will set
free the enemies who have harmed me and all of us,
who have created obstacles that harm us, obstacles
to liberation and omniscience; and I will set free
Mara and the assembly of Mara.

I will set free those who are imprisoned in samsara. I will establish in the mahamudra those who
are not established in the mahamudra. Those who
have not attained nirvana I will establish in nirvana.

In *Engaging in the Bodhisattva Deeds*, Shāntideva wrote:

If those who are stricken — bound by the prison of
cyclic existence — generate bodhichitta, then, from
that instant, they are called Bodhisattvas, and they
become the object of true respect in the worlds of
gods and human beings.

Furthermore, the Buddha said:

> There is one quality which, if possessed by the
> Bodhisattvas, enables them to abandon the lower
> realms and not to consort with evil friends; it en-
> ables them to attain completely perfect Buddha-
> hood quickly. What is that quality? It is the mind of
> enlightenment, the perfection of the unusual atti-
> tude.

Actual Bodhichitta

If one does not have the second, the actual mind of enlightenment, one will not bring to completion the first, the
aspirational mind of enlightenment. Atīsha said:

> If you generate the aspirational mind
> But do not cultivate the three ethics,[41]
> You will not attain enlightenment.
> To cultivate these ethics well —
> That is the vow of the Bodhisattva.
> Therefore, exert yourself
> To fulfill the Bodhisattva vow.

Atīsha also said:

> If you have not fulfilled the vow of the actual mind
> of enlightenment, the aspirational mind will not be
> increased. Thus, if you wish to increase the aspir-
> ational mind of enlightenment and bring it to com-
> pletion, you must diligently practice this actual
> mind of enlightenment.

The Object of Observation of Actual Bodhichitta

Make a firm promise, thinking:

> So that all sentient beings may attain Buddhahood,
> from this time until tomorrow, until the end of my
> life, and until I attain enlightenment, I will perform
> virtuous deeds of body, speech, and mind. From
> now until then I will practice the stages of the

profound fivefold path.

Making this promise firmly is the conventional mind of enlightenment. Setting one's mind on emptiness is the ultimate mind of enlightenment. These two bring forth virtues without ceasing. There are several comments on this in *Engaging in the Bodhisattva Deeds:*

> All other virtues produce fruit just once
> And then are exhausted,
> Like a banana tree;
> But the tree of bodhichitta
> Bears fruit endlessly,
> Increasing without end.

> The aspirational mind of enlightenment
> Brings forth great fruit in cyclic existence;
> But it does not bring forth virtue ceaselessly,
> As does the actual mind of enlightenment.

> To set completely free
> The myriad sentient beings in all the realms,
> You must permanently attain a mind of
>   enlightenment.
> If you have such a nonreversable mind,
> Then — from the time of its first arising,
> And whether you are awake or asleep —
> The force of its merit wells up continuously,
> Completely filling all of space.

Those who generate bodhichitta achieve their purpose ceaselessly and benefit others in whatever way they wish.

From our initial aspiration (for the good qualities to be achieved through practice) until we attain the Truth Body, we should pay homage to Vajradhara, thinking, in the words of Nāgārjuna:

> I bow down to the glorious Vajradhara,
> The Nature Body of the mind of enlightenment.

This is how the ultimate is attained.

ACTUAL PRACTICES
Meditation on Yidam, the essence of Secret Mantra
Meditation on the Teacher, the essence of knowledge
Meditation on Mahamudra, the essence of the meaning

Meditation on Yidam — Deity Yoga

The meditation on the yidam deity has two stages: generation and completion. The *Guhyasamāja Tantra* says:

> For the one who wants to maintain the stage of generation and attain the stage of completion, the supreme Buddha taught this method, like the steps of a ladder.

This profound fivefold path of mahamudra is the stage of completion of a mother tantra.[42] Thus, when practicing the stage of generation in the yidam meditation, one must also cultivate a mother tantra, in this case the innate Chakrasamvara Tantra involving one male deity. And when practicing the stage of completion, one must cultivate the yoga of subtle drops, the four bodies, the eight signs, the channels and winds, and so forth.[43]

For practicing the stage of generation, Lord Jigten Sumgön said:

> If you have not established firmly your body as that of the yidam diety, then the retinue of mother Dakinis will not assemble. Thus, firmly establish your body as yidam.

Venerable Tilopa said:

> The explanation of the mode of abiding of reality
> has two parts: the way to practice the path and the
> stages of generation of the fruit.

From another point of view, the explanation of the mode
of abiding of reality has two parts, explaining the mode of
abiding of the body and of the mind. The mode of abiding
of the body is based on the five perfections. Associated with
the five perfections are the five wisdoms.[44] These are, the
Hevajra Tantra says:

> From the moon, the mirror-like exalted wisdom;
> from the sun, the exalted wisdom of sameness; from
> the seed syllable of the deity and the hand symbol,
> the exalted wisdom of individual realization; with
> the completed stage of generation, the exalted wis-
> dom of achieving activities; and with the stage of
> completion — the exalted wisdom of the element of
> qualities.[45]
>
> Scholars tell us that we are to generate the five
> perfections: the perfection from the basis — empti-
> ness; the perfection from the seats of sun and moon
> discs; the perfection from the symbols of the wis-
> dom mind; the perfection from the syllables, which
> are the symbols of speech; and the perfection from
> the complete body.

THE STAGE OF GENERATION

This stage[46] involves the cultivation of the five perfections.
First, generate a conventional mind of enlightenment,
thinking:

> I will lead all sentient beings — the mothers, limit-
> less as space — to the attainment of the rank of
> Vajradhara.

Then, generate an ultimate mind of enlightenment,

thinking:

> *Oṃ svabhawa shuddha sarva dharma svabhawa*
> *shuddho hang.*[47]
> All phenomena become emptiness, which is pure by
> nature.

That is the perfection from the basis — emptiness.

The other four perfections are generated in this way:
from within emptiness there arise, one above the other, the
syllable *yaṃ*, which becomes a wind mandala; the syllable
raṃ, which becomes a fire mandala; *baṃ*, which becomes a
water mandala; *laṃ*, which becomes an earth mandala; *suṃ*,
which becomes Mount Meru; *paṃ*, which becomes a hun-
dred-thousand-petalled variegated lotus; *āḥ* and *raṃ*, which
become the seats of sun and moon.

On the sun and moon there is a blue five-spoke vajra, in
the center of which is a syllable *hūṃ*. The hand symbol —
the blue vajra — symbolizes the wisdom mind; the *hūṃ*
symbolizes speech. From the syllable *hūṃ*, light radiates; it
fulfills the two purposes — of yourself and others — and
then returns to the *hūṃ* in the vajra. Through the complete
transformation of the vajra and syllable *hūṃ*, you become
Chakrasamvara, in clear male and female aspects. This is
the fifth perfection, through the completed body.

Visualization
One must visualize in sequence the face, color, and so on, of
Chakrasamvara. Then, having held oneself as these, one
dissolves them back into oneself. This is the meaning of the
Hevajra Tantra, when it says: "Generation of face, hand,
color; from their mere production, they abide."

Meditate in the following way: visualize yourself to be the
blue male Heruka,[48] blue like the color of the stainless sky,
with one face and two hands, holding vajra and bell. At the
top of the hair knot at the crown of his head is a wish-
fulfilling wisdom jewel. On top of this is a five-spoke vajra;
to the left of the vajra is a crescent moon. Heruka's head is

adorned with five dry skulls. From his neck hangs a necklace of human intestine, on which are hung 51 fresh human heads, dripping blood. He is adorned with six symbols and six bone ornaments;[49] his lower garment is of tiger skin. His outstretched right leg is planted between the breasts of Dutsen and his left-foot is pressed against the head of Jikche. He makes the nine gestures: the three of body — graceful, heroic, and ugly; the three of speech — laughing, fierce, and frightening; the three of mind — compassionate, frightful, and peaceful.

Meditate on yourself as Heruka having these nine gestures. On his lap is the female Vajrayogini of red color, with two faces. Her hair is swept up onto the crown of her head. Upon it is a half vajra; a tassel falls behind her from her head to her feet. Her main face is a fierce one, with three eyes and clenched bared teeth; she sips the honey of Heruka's lips. Behind her right ear is the face of a pig; by its rumbling noises, she overwhelms the three realms and outshines the three existences. Vajrayogini holds in her right hand a curved knife which extends to Heruka's left shoulder. Her left arm is around his neck; her left hand holds a skull-cup full of blood, which she offers to Heruka. She wears a head ornament of five dry skulls, a fresh garland of human heads, as well as five symbols and bone ornaments.[50] Beside Heruka's right foot, her left foot also is planted between the breasts of Dutsen. Her right leg is around Heruka's waist. On the forehead of each, there is the syllable *oṃ;* at their throats, *āḥ;* at his heart, *hūṃ;* at her heart, *baṃ.*

From each syllable, light radiates, inviting actual wisdom-beings like the ones you have visualized; they appear and become one with the pledge-being.[51] Again, light radiates from the syllables, inviting the Buddhas of the five lineages or families.[52] They appear and bestow empowerments, filling your body (visualized as one with Heruka) with wisdom nectar, cleansing all stains. Overflowing, the wisdom nectar turns into the Buddha Akshobhya above your head and turns into Vairochana above the head of Vajrayogini. The Buddhas of the five lineages then dissolve into you.

The *Guhyasamāja Tantra* says:

> You are to establish yourself completely; that is, as all Buddhas and Conquerors, as Dakas and Dakinis, and as all Bodhisattvas.

In this way, the three seats are completed.[53]

The blessings we need are of the body and of speech. As to the blessing of one's body, it is said that the nature of the form aggregate is Vairochana; the nature of the feeling aggregate is Dorje Nyima; that of the discrimination aggregate is Pema Gargi Wangchuk; that of the aggregate of compositional factors is Dorje Gyalpo; and that of the aggregate of consciousness is Vajrasattva. The nature of oneself as yidam is the five Buddha lineages.

A visualization accompanies the blessing of one's body: At the navel of Vajrayogini is a red Dorjepakmo; at her heart is a blue Shinjema; at her throat is a white Monchyema; at her forehead, a yellow Gyonchema; at the crown of her head, a green Trakchema; and at all of her limbs, smoky colored Tsantikas. Heruka and Vajrayogini each have 12 protection deities.

To receive the blessing of speech, one should recite the mantras which are the essence and inner essence of Heruka and Vajrayogini in father and mother aspect. The mantra that is the essence of Heruka is: *"Oṃ shrī vazra he he ru ru kam hūng hūng phaṭ; ḍākini zwala saṃwaraṃ svāhā.* His inner essence is: *"Oṃ hrī ha ha hūng hūng phaṭ."* The essence-mantra of Vajrayogini is: *"Oṃ oṃ oṃ sarva Buddha ḍākiniye; vazra warnaniye; vazra verotsaniye; hūng hūng hūng phaṭ phaṭ phaṭ svāhā."* Her inner essence is, *"Oṃ vazraverotsanī hūng phaṭ."*[54] If you become tired of reciting, then set your mind on the meaning of the meditation.

Commentary on the Stage of Generation
There are three different assertions with regard to this
stage. Some say it is imaginary, some that it is other-
powered, and still others that it is thoroughly established.
From the point of view of our own system, the stage of
generation is not imaginary. This is because if the stage did
not actually exist in some way, then the visualization would
have no power; and it does have power. Furthermore, from
our point of view, the stage of generation is not just other-
powered, because it does not always depend on other conditions. We hold that the stage of generation is thoroughly
established.[55]

The *Guhyasamāja Tantra* says:

> In brief, it is to be known that the five aggregates
> are the five Buddhas; it is to be known that the 12
> vajra sources are the supreme mandala of Bodhisatt-
> vas, the earth element is Buddha Lochana, the wa-
> ter element is Mamaki, the fire element is white
> Pandara Vasini, and the wind element is Samaya
> Tara. It is to be ascertained that all forms, sounds,
> tastes, and so forth are tantric deities.

To meditate on the meaning of this, one can follow three
mental practices: 1) meditation on the clear form;
2) mindfulness of the purity of the form; and 3) holding
firmly to the diamond-perfection[56] of oneself as deity.[57]

1. Meditation on the Clear Form

The clear (or luminous) form is not the composite form of
flesh and blood. The clear form (or body) is to be understood as the three of 12 examples of illusion.[58] Nāgārjuna
says:

> In your body is no empty space,
> No flesh or blood or bone,
> No sense of thirst or hunger,
> No pure or impure parts;
> See it as like a rainbow in the sky.

In the *Ḍākinī Vajrapañjara Tantra,* the Buddha says:

> Whoever meditates on my body as being like an illusory form or as being like a dream has the pure practice; becoming thoroughly familiar with this, such a practitioner will see me directly.

And Glorious Phagmo Drupa says:

> We meditate on the body of the deity as being like a rainbow in order to abandon the conception of ordinariness.[59]

Therefore, meditate on the clear appearance of the deity as being without true existence, like a rainbow.

2. Mindfulness of the purity of the form

The practice of mindfulness of the purity of the form has two variants, the purity of the natural signs (the Form Body) and the purity of emptiness (the Truth Body). These are the meaning of merit and wisdom, the causes.[60]

a) Mindfulness of the purity of the natural signs. The *Hevajra Tantra* says:

> At the crown of the head of the visualized deity is Akshobhya; at the throat is Ratnasambhava; at the hand is Vairochana; at the waist is Amoghasiddhi; at the arms and legs are Vajrasattva

Thus one meditates on the meaning of the deity (Heruka) as adorned by the six ornaments. Think that the substance of each of the deity's ornaments is pure. In this way you will attain each fruit of Buddhahood — separation and ripening.[61] If your meditation is not steady, then gaps and faults will arise, and the fruit will not arise.

b) Mindfulness of the purity that is emptiness. Nāropa said:

> Appearance and emptiness —
> Emptiness and appearance;
> Discern these as nondual,

Like the moon in water.

This reminds us that we must know the stage of generation to be without true existence. If we forget this, we will become attached to the special appearance — having abandoned ordinary appearance.

3. Holding firmly to the diamond-perfection of oneself as deity

This is an unswerving attention to the perfection of the deity, likened to a diamond in purity and adamantine firmness, and unswerving attention to oneself as that deity.[62] In following this practice, one must hold all appearances to be the body of the deity, hold all sound to be the speech of the deity, and hold all minds to be the mind of the deity. The *Hevajra Tantra* says:

> If one is following this method of mental practice —
> the yoga of selflessness, the effort of Heruka — then
> even one moment of another practice will prevent
> attainment of the fruit.

THE STAGE OF COMPLETION

If the meditator enters the clear light by the process of gradual dissolving after meditating on nontrue existence, then at the end of the session, he or she collects everything into emptiness.

The *Guhyasamāja Tantra* says:

> Everything from the crown of the head to the feet
> dissolves into the heart; you engage in the perfect
> yoga (meditation on emptiness). This is the stage
> called complete holding. All sentient beings and all
> other phenomena dissolve into clear light and then
> dissolve into you; then you yourself, as the deity,
> dissolve into your heart. This is the stage called
> post-dissolution. Just as mist on a mirror fades to-
> ward the center and disappears, so does everything

— the net of illusory manifestation — dissolve into the clear light of emptiness. Just as fish are easily seen in clear water, so does everything — the net of illusory manifestation — emerge from the clear light of emptiness.

By the light of the mind, shining in your heart, all phenomena and sentient beings come together and dissolve into you.[63] Your base (the lion, throne, sun, moon, and so forth) and you yourself dissolve into the syllable *hūṃ* at your heart. Then the *hūṃ* also dissolves: the vowel mark *u* dissolves into the root letter *ha*, which dissolves into the top line of the letter, which in turn dissolves into the curved line above it; that then dissolves into the circle, which dissolves into the curl at the top. The curl splits into a hundred thousand fragments, each of which dissolves until the whole syllable has dissolved into emptiness.

Observe that emptiness. Be aware of it. Experience the equal taste of all phenomena in emptiness.

Meditation on the Teacher — Guru Yoga

There is only one way to generate in one's mind the completion stage; this way is guru yoga, the profound path.[64] The *Hevajra Tantra* says:

> Inexpressible innate wisdom is found only in the base — highest devotion to the guru — and in one's own merit.

Tilopa says:

> The ignorant may know that sesame oil — the essence — exists in the sesame seed, but because they do not know how, they cannot extract the oil. So also does innate fundamental wisdom abide in the heart of all migrators; but unless it is pointed out by the guru, it cannot be realized. By pounding the seeds and clearing away the husks, one can extract the essence — the sesame oil. Similarly, when it is shown by the lama, the meaning of suchness is so illuminated that one can enter into it.

The *Atiköpa Tantra* says:

> If you meditate on your kind lama

At the crown of your head,
Or in the palm of your hand,
Or at the center of your heart—
You will possess the good qualities
Of the thousand Buddhas.

Furthermore, the *Damtsikōpa Tantra* says:

Even if you practice the stage of completion for an
aeon, this cannot equal in power the appearance of
the guru in your heart for even the tiniest fraction of
a moment. Practice guru yoga without distraction,
and the lama will appear in the center of your heart.
The guru's appearing there — even for just an
instant — is so powerful that if it is divided two
million times, the strength of a single part of it still
cannot be matched by the stage of completion.

And the *Guhyasamāja Tantra* says:

By meditating on the guru at the heart,
One attains the mind of enlightenment.
By this marvelous accomplishment
The body, speech, and mind of a Buddha are
established.

Lord Jigten Sumgön says:

If, on the snow mountain of the guru's four bodies,[65]
The sun of your devotion does not shine,
The stream of blessings will not arise;
Attend, therefore, to this mind of devotion.

This means that:

I. The outwardly established Emanation Body is established as activity (activity engaged in for the sake of others);

II. The inwardly established Complete Enjoyment Body
is established as good qualities (good qualities that one
possesses oneself);

III. The secretly established Truth Body is established as
nonduality; and

IV. Suchness is established as the Nature Body.

I. THE EMANATION BODY

Glorious Phagmo Drupa tells us how to establish the first, the outwardly established Emanation Body, as activity:

> Invite to the space before you the root lama — the Supramundane Victor — and the assembly of the Buddhas and Bodhisattvas of the three times. The root lama sits in the aspect of the Buddha on the throne of the lion, lotus, and sun and moon disc seat. Offer the sevenfold prayer, as well as your body and your possessions. Visualize yourself as inseparable from the root lama. Say the prayers, going for refuge respectfully with the special qualities. Repeat the prayer-mantra (to the Emanation Body).[66] Set your mind in the state free from the three conceptions.

Meditate: in the space before you, having the divine pride of yourself as the yidam deity, is a precious throne held up by eight blue lions. On it is a lotus, on top of which are discs of sun and moon; above these is the guru, the Lord of Teaching, the Supramundane Victor, the Conqueror Shakyamuni. The brilliant gold of his body is touched with red. He has one face and two hands; his right hand presses the earth, and his left is in the meditative posture, holding a begging bowl filled with precious jewels. He wears the three dharma robes of saffron color. A crown-protrusion rises from his head but is not visible.[67] He is adorned with the precious major and minor marks of a Buddha. He sits in the cross-legged vajra posture, radiating light.

This is the outwardly established Emanation Body, to whom you will next give homage, the three offerings, and the sevenfold offering.

The Three Branches of Homage
These are: 1) the offering of the visualized body of the deity; 2) the offering of praise; and 3) prostration.

1) Viewing the body of the deity before you, as described, look at it and generate faith and respect. Then think, "How happy I am to meet with the deities."

2) Offer praise, thinking:

I offer praise to you, the Supreme Protector.
Yours is the complete form, pure and beautiful.
Your fame shines, illuminating the universe.

Or think:

Praise to the embodiment of all the Buddhas,
The entity of the holder of the vajra,
Root of the Three Jewels, the Supreme Lama.

Offer this same praise to all Four Buddha Bodies.

Within this homage are included a) the ethics of accumulating virtue, b) the ethics for the sake of sentient beings, and c) the ethics of vows. It is the special teaching of Lord Jigten Sumgön that in any one virtue — or any portion or moment of the branches of homage—these three ethics can be discerned:

a) Ethics of accumulating virtue: prostration through emanations of one's body, as many as the particles of dust.
b) Ethics for the sake of sentient beings: prostrations for the benefit of sentient beings.
c) Ethics of vows: establishing the harmonious conditions of prostration and abandoning contrary conditions.[68]

3) Offer the homage of prostration, saying:

Namo guru Buddha dharma saṅgha Bodhisattvabhye.

The Threefold Offering
Viewing the deity, visualized as described, make the three offerings: outer, inner, and secret.

1) The outer offerings are those established from the substance of the gods.[69] Actually lay out the eight offerings of

Samantabhadra and then offer them mentally. Perform these offerings while maintaining the three ethics.[70]

2) Next make the inner offering. Think that from the seed syllable at your heart there emanate five types of offering goddesses — goddesses of vajra-sound, sight, odor, taste, and tangibility. They emanate just as one flame becomes two, and three, and more.[71] These goddesses make offerings of bliss and emptiness to the assembled Buddhas and Bodhisattvas.

3) Next make the secret offering, the ultimate offering. This is emptiness, which is the nonobservation of action, object, and agent. This emptiness is never-ending.

The Sevenfold Offering
Still viewing the body of the deity as before, perform the seven-branched offering:

> Prostrating oneself,
> Offering,
> Confessing of wrongdoing,
> Rejoicing in the virtue of others,
> Asking the teacher to turn the wheel of dharma,
> Praying that one will not go into the state of nirvana,
> Aspiring to enlightenment and dedicating virtue.

This is the branch of asking the teacher to turn the wheel of dharma: manifest your body in as many manifestations as there are particles of dust; then have each of those emanations offer a golden wheel; each wheel has a thousand spokes. Offer these to the visualized deity and make a verbal offering, saying:

> May the sound of the dharma drum
> Free all sentient beings from suffering.
> Please stay for limitless aeons,
> Teaching the precious doctrine.

Direct these seven pure offerings, as well as the three branches of homage and the threefold offering, to all Four Buddha Bodies.

Then, pray to the outwardly established Emanation Body, saying:

I pray to the form of the Precious Lama, who is the entity of the bodies of all the Buddhas of the three times.

I pray to the voice of the Precious Lama, who is the entity of the speech of all the Buddhas of the three times.

I pray to the mind — the exalted wisdom — of the Precious Lama, who is the entity of the minds of all the Buddhas of the three times.

Then the assembly of deities in front of you dissolves into you. Keep your mind in the natural state without having any thought at all.[72]

When arising from this meditative session, dedicate the merit to the welfare of all sentient beings.

II. THE COMPLETE ENJOYMENT BODY

These are the instructions of Phagmo Drupa for establishing the inwardly established Complete Enjoyment Body as good qualities:

Then, the assembly of deities manifesting in the space before you dissolves into you[73] and you become the body of the yidam. The lotus at the heart center blossoms, and on the seat of the sun and moon discs is the wish-fulfilling gem, the body of the Ultimate Lama appearing as Vairochana, the Complete Enjoyment Body. He radiates light. At the three special places of Vairochana (forehead, throat, and heart) are the seats of moon, lotus, and sun. Place the three syllables *oṃ, āḥ,* and *hūṃ* at these places — the centers of body, speech, and mind. The three fruits (Buddha Body, Buddha Speech, and Buddha Mind) arise, and the pure light from those three centers of Vairochana radiates to the three realms; the beings of the three realms thereby attain pure bodies, inseparable from those of the Buddha.

Then all that you have visualized dissolves into Vairochana as a mandala of light. Repeat the prayer-mantra (of the Kagyu lamas)[74] without wavering from the meditative state. Think that everything dissolves into a state of nonduality forever free of the three conceptions.

This means that, having dissolved the Emanation Body into yourself, you are then to meditate, visualizing the following:

The substance at the center of your heart is a precious throne, held up by eight blue lions. Visualize that the eight channels of your heart are an eight-petalled lotus on the throne. Visualize the white substance in your heart as a moon disc and the red as a sun disc; above them sits the excellent Lama Vairochana, in whose body all realms are reflected and whose body pervades all realms. From his body, light radiates. He is endowed with a Complete Enjoyment Body. Think that on the moon at his forehead there is a white *oṃ*. On the lotus at his throat there is a red *āḥ*. On the sun at his heart there is a blue *hūṃ*. Around the *hūṃ* are the secret names of the Kagyu lamas.

Offer the verbal prayer-mantra of the Kagyu lamas:

> *Om ah namo guru vazra dhrika mahamudra siddhi phala hung*
>
> *Om ah namo guru prajnabhadra mahamudra siddhi phala hung*
>
> *Om ah namo guru jnana siddhi mahamudra siddhi phala hung*
>
> *Om ah namo guru dharma mati mahamudra siddhi phala hung*
>
> *Om ah namo guru vazra dwaza mahamudra siddhi phala hung*
>
> *Om ah namo guru zambudvipa kirti mahamudra siddhi phala hung*

*Om ah namo guru vazra raza mahamudra siddhi
phala hung*

*Om ah namo guru trilokya natha ratna shri maha-
mudra siddhi phala hung*

*Om ah namo guru upadeya shila vazra mahamudra
siddhi phala hung*

*Om ah namo guru punye kirti mahamudra siddhi
phala hung*

*Om ah namo guru kirti kara mahamudra siddhi phala
hung*

*Om ah namo guru vazra kirti mahamudra siddhi
phala hung*

*Om ah namo guru ratna singha mahamudra siddhi
phala hung*

*Om ah namo guru kirti punya mahamudra siddhi
phala hung*

*Om ah namo guru vazra ratna mahamudra siddhi
phala hung*

*Om ah namo guru vazra raza mahamudra siddhi
phala hung*

*Om ah namo guru zambudvipa dharma raza
mahamudra siddhi phala hung*

*Om ah namo guru artha siddhi raza mahamudra
siddhi phala hung*

*Om ah namo guru ratna shri sya dwaza mahamudra
siddhi phala hung*

*Om ah namo guru dharma raza ratna shri bhadra
mahamudra siddhi phala hung*

*Om ah namo guru ratna dharma sya dwaza
mahamudra siddhi phala hung*

*Om ah namo guru ratna dharma raza mahamudra
siddhi phala hung*

*Om ah namo guru sarvajna ananta ratna dharma
sya dwaza shri bhadra mahamudra siddhi phala
hung*

*Om ah namo guru zayandra ratna sampanna maha-
mudra siddhi phala hung*

Om ah namo guru punya shri sya sagara mahamudra siddhi phala hung

Om ah namo guru dharma raza lakshim mangala shri bhadra mahamudra siddhi phala hung

Om ah namo guru mangala sampanna kirti dwaza shri bhadra mahamudra siddhi phala hung

Om ah namo guru vazra akshobhya mahamudra siddhi phala hung

Om ah namo guru dharma kirti karma vizaya sena mahamudra siddhi phala hung

Om ah namo guru ratna karma vizaya mahamudra siddhi phala hung

Om ah namo guru ratna karma bhadra mahamudra siddhi phala hung

Om ah namo guru ratna karma artha siddhi dharma raza mahamudra siddhi phala hung

Om ah namo guru ratna shasanadhara gadharshi mahamudra siddhi phala hung

Om ah namo guru ratna dharma dwaza mahamudra siddhi phala hung

Om ah namo guru dharma surya mahamudra siddhi phala hung

Om ah namo guru padma sya dwaza mahamudra siddhi phala hung

Om ah namo guru dharma sya dwaza mahamudra siddhi phala hung

Om ah namo guru vidyadhara mati dwaza mahamudra siddhi phala hung

Om ah namo guru dharmema mani shri bhadra mahamudra siddhi phala hung

Om ah namo guru ratna karunya sya surya mahamudra siddhi phala hung

Om ah namo guru ratna shasana dwaza mahamudra siddhi phala hung

Om ah namo guru shasana dhara dharma mati karma vizaya shri bhadra mahamudra siddhi phala hung

Om ah namo guru ratna muni shasana shanta mati karma vizaya shri bhadra mahamudra siddhi phala hung

Then pray to the Lama Vairochana at your heart:

> Crowned wish-fulfilling Lord, mind of the Con-
> queror, beyond words, thoughts, and expression,
> having the five exalted wisdoms; compassionate Lord
> of Kindness, precious Protector of Migrators, I pray
> to you from the depths of my heart. Please bestow
> blessings from within emptiness. Please bestow bless-
> ings on me, that I may realize the Truth Body, be-
> yond conceptual thought — this pure innate mind,
> unproduced and existing from the beginning.

Make this prayer very strongly, with a one-pointed mind.
By the power of this prayer, light radiates from the garland
of mantras surrounding the seed syllables of the body,
speech, and mind of Vairochana. The light touches all
sentient beings in the three realms, causing all their faults
and obstructions to vanish; then it returns and dissolves
into the lama. Then the lama also melts into light and dissolves into the syllable *hūṃ* at his heart. The syllable *hūṃ*
also dissolves, as before: the vowel mark *u* dissolves into
the root letter *ha*, which dissolves into the top line of the
letter, which in turn dissolves into the curved line above it;
that then dissolves into the circle, which dissolves into the
curl at the top. The curl splits into a hundred thousand
fragments, each of which dissolves until the whole syllable
has dissolved into emptiness.[75] Set your mind in the
nonduality of the mahamudra state.

Arising from this meditation, dedicate the merit to all
sentient beings.

III. THE TRUTH BODY

With regard to the establishment of the Truth Body as
nonduality, Lord Jigten Sumgön says:

> In a supreme Pure Land at the crown of your head,
> there appears, according to the needs of sentient
> beings, a Complete Enjoyment Body — union of

great bliss and emptiness, simultaneously free from expression and conditions.

Offer the sevenfold offering, as well as your form and possessions, to the great Vajradhara with the three bodies and seven qualities; light then radiates from his centers and spreads to the Buddha fields. Invite the innumerable emanations of Vajradhara; after appearing, they all dissolve back into the heart-center of Vajradhara.

Maintaining a state of meditative stability, repeat the prayer-mantra[76] invoking the body, speech, and mind of Vajradhara. Then all the visualized deities dissolve into you. Think that you are completely free of the three conceptions.

This means that you are to visualize at the crown of your head a precious throne held up by eight lions; on it are a lotus and the discs of sun and moon; on top of these sits the lama, Vajradhara, whose body is as blue as a lapis lazuli jewel touched by the light of the sun. He has one face and two hands, holding vajra and bell at his heart. He has two legs and is seated in the vajra posture. Fully adorned with the major and minor marks of a Buddha, he radiates light.

At the forehead of this visualized Vajradhara, endowed with the Complete Enjoyment Body, is the syllable *oṃ*; at his throat is the letter *āḥ*; at his heart, the syllable *hūṃ*. Light radiates from these. Invite the lama, the yidam deities, the Buddhas, Bodhisattvas, Dakas, Dakinis, and Dharma Protectors to the space in front of you. Having appeared, they all then dissolve into the lama, Vajradhara. Meditate then on the lama as the embodiment of all the objects of refuge. Make the seven pure offerings along with the mandala offering. This is the prayer-mantra you are to repeat:

Homage to the Lama. Please bestow blessings on me that there may arise in me the special realization of my own body, speech, and mind as inseparable from those of the lama, whose body, speech, and mind—spontaneous and unceasing—pervade cyclic existence and nirvana in the past, present, and future.

The first empowerment. Recite: "Glorious Lama, embodiment of all good qualities, please enter the opening in the center of the crown of my head. Please purify the tendencies of the waking state with the water of the vase empowerment of delight." By the power of this prayer, white light radiates from the *om* at the Lama's forehead and dissolves into your forehead, purifying the obscurations of the waking state. You obtain the vase empowerment and the Emanation Body, which is Vajra Form.

The second empowerment. Recite: "Language of all sentient beings, the Complete Enjoyment Body, please enter the center of speech at my throat. May the duality of dreams be burnt by the fire of the secret empowerment of supreme joy." By the power of this prayer, red light radiates from the letter *āḥ* at the throat of the precious Lama and dissolves into your throat, purifying the obscurations of the dream state. You obtain the secret empowerment and the Complete Enjoyment Body, which is Vajra Speech.

The third empowerment. Recite: "Body of the saintly, precious Lama, the nonconceptual Dharmakaya, please enter into the center of my mind at the heart, and awaken the dark thickness of sleep with the primordial wisdom awareness." By the power of this prayer, blue light radiates from the *hūṃ* at the heart of the precious Lama and dissolves into your heart, purifying the obscurations of deep sleep. You obtain the wisdom empowerment and the Truth Body, which is Vajra Mind.

The fourth empowerment. Recite: "Lord of sentient beings, the co-emergent awareness body, please enter the center of primordial awareness at my navel. May I obtain unchanging joy by the empowerment of great wisdom awareness." By the power of this prayer, yellow light radiates from the navel of the precious Lama and dissolves into your navel, purifying the obscurations of movement. You obtain the fourth empowerment and the Nature Body, which is Vajra Wisdom.

Recite: "May the body, speech, mind and primordial wisdom of myself and sentient beings equal to space unite equally with your four Vajras, and attain the Supreme Joy." By the power of this prayer, the precious Lama melts into a ray of light and dissolves into you. Your body, speech, and mind become inseparable from the Lama's body, speech, and mind. Set your mind in the meditative absorption of the state of nonduality.

In the *Ocean of Wisdom Sutra*, Buddha said:

> From the centers of the lama's body, receive completely the four empowerments. This is the essential meaning of the tantras. One who receives these empowerments will accomplish all of the stages of the ten grounds and five paths,[77] without exception.

Then set your mind in the natural, nonartificial state. When you arise from the meditative session, dedicate the merit to the welfare of all sentient beings.

IV. THE NATURE BODY

With regard to the establishment of suchness as the Nature Body, Phagmo Drupa said:

> The ultimate nature of the mind beyond thought is the Truth Body, spontaneous natural luminosity and suchness, which from the beginning is pure, unproduced, and unconditioned. Now—undefiled by the stains of conceptuality and in the peaceful state of great bliss, nonconceptual and uncontaminated—abandon the effort of meditation. Abandon the conception of object of meditation and meditator. Place your mind at rest in the natural, nonartificial state, without effort.
>
> The great, inexpressible, inconceivable mahamudra is the Precious Lama, inseparable from the Four Buddha Bodies. The lama is victorious over Mara and the afflictions, and is the embodiment of the infinite ocean of good qualities. The Buddha called this the highest accomplishment.

Meditate on the meaning of that.[78] Meditating in such a way, you will come to understand that your own mind is, in its very nature, the precious Lama.

Make the seven pure offerings along with the mandala offering. Then pray, thinking:

> Precious Lama, the Truth Body, spontaneous and unconditioned, please bestow on me the empowerments of your body, speech, mind, and good qualities and activities.

Pay no attention to external objects; do not perform mental actions, either. Be unstained by even the slightest thought conceiving the act of meditation. Relax your body, speech, and mind into their own nature.

This practice merges the two into one: the great mahamudra, the pure basic mind that abides from the beginning, can no longer be distinguished from the ever-arising thought, and the thought perceives nothing but that basic mind as the lama. The two are inseparable, like water mixed with water, butter with butter.

Now nothing whatever remains of your own body, speech, and mind. The four bodies of the lama—the Truth Body without production, the Complete Enjoyment Body without cessation, the Emanation Body without abiding, the Nature Body inseparable from the other three—are completed in your own mind.

Lord Jigten Sumgön says:

> Emptiness, the nature of the basic mind, is the Truth Body. That which is clear and unceasing is the Complete Enjoyment Body. Manifestation, various and without duality, is the Emanation Body. Thus, phenomena are one, undifferentiable. That indivisible oneness of phenomena is the essential nature of reality (the Nature Body).

When you arise from meditation, do the dedication, free from the three spheres of conceptuality.

Meditation on Mahamudra

With regard to the practice of mahamudra, the essence of
the meaning, Lord Jigten Sumgön says:

> If, in the vast sky of the basic mind,
> The clouds of conceptuality are not cleared away,
> The planets and stars of the two wisdoms will not
>   shine.
> Attend, therefore, to this mind free of dualistic
>   perception.[79]

The sky symbolizes the basic mind; the planets (sun and
moon) and stars symbolize the two wisdoms as well as the
fruit — the Buddha qualities of separation and ripening.
Cloud and fog symbolize afflictions and conceptions. Just as
the clouds and fog prevent the sun, moon, and stars from
shining, so the three obstructions[80] prevent the exalted
wisdom from manifesting.

To clear away the three obstructions, one must thoroughly purify one's view,[81] one's meditation, and one's activities. There are two possible approaches: finding the view
first and then practicing meditation; or meditating first and
then finding the view. According to Lord Jigten Sumgön,
one first establishes the foundation — the view.[82] Nāropa

says:

> If your understanding does not accord exactly with
> the correct view, as it has been shown by the lama,
> then your view and your actions will be mistaken.
> You will be as if blind and without a guide; thus you
> will not attain the fruit.

It is necessary to settle the view,[83] to carefully delineate the
view.

SETTLING THE VIEW

There are many ways of asserting the view; all holders of
tenets assert the view in their own way. There are some,
however, who have the view but do not have realization.
They are depending on their own power alone, and will find
it difficult to go any farther in their understanding. Lord
Jigten Sumgön says:

> Those people do indeed have many ways of assert-
> ing the view, but they do not have the realization
> that arises from meditation. Therefore, theirs is a
> view lacking realization.

The view must be accompanied by realization. There must
be realization of the meaning (mahamudra); that is, there
must be direct experience — beyond thought — of the
meaning.
  Through the view, the meaning is established; through
meditation, the meaning is experienced; through activities,
the experience of the meaning is enhanced. The fruit is
already there; its attaining must simply be a discovering.
Nāropa said: "Extract and delineate the meaning."

SETTLING THE TRUE NATURE OF THE MIND

To understand the mode of abiding of the mind, one must
analyze both the mode of abiding of appearances (all objects) and the mode of abiding of minds (all subjects).

The Mode of Abiding of Appearances
First, it is established that conventional appearances are the mind itself. Nāropa said:

> The fact that these appearing and occurring phenomena (all objects) appear and are illuminated means that they do not exist apart from the mind of self-awareness. Just as self-awareness is an experience of the mind knowing itself, so whatever appears is an experience of the self-awareness (or consciousness) that perceives it. If the mind and these phenomena are not the same, then the phenomena must be totally different from the mind and can have no relationship with the mind. Without a relationship between them, phenomena would not appear to mind. This is the way we delineate the conventional existence of phenomena.

Thus, all phenomena are understood as being one's own mind.

The Mode of Abiding of the Mind
The mind must be understood to be without basis, without foundation. Nāropa said:

> The Buddha said, 'all phenomena abide in the mind.' The actual basis of phenomena is the mind itself. If one analyses the nature of the mind — by the four reasonings, and so forth — it is found to have the two stains of conceptuality.[84] The teaching of the reasoning of one and many has a meaning that is very profound and thus is to be analyzed by the wise.

THE FOUR REASONINGS

To determine that the mind of self-awareness is without true existence, we use four great reasons — the four reasonings. The way of identifying the four reasonings here differs slightly from the way they are identified in the Madhyamika literature. These are the four reasonings: analysis of the cause, the reasoning of the diamond slivers; analysis of the entity, the reasoning of one and many; analysis of the effect, the reasoning refuting the four possibilities of production; and analysis of all phenomena, the reasoning of dependent-arising.[85]

1. The Reasoning of the Diamond Slivers
The way in which effects arise from actions (causes) is similar to the way sprouts arise from seeds. Nāgārjuna said in his *Treatise on the Middle Way:*

> There is never production
> Anywhere, of any thing
> From itself, from others,
> From both, or without cause.

In that same way, appearances and minds are shown to be without basis, without foundation. Thus one understands the ultimate nature of the mind.

2. The Reasoning of One and Many
If one mentally divides a thing into tiny parts, it can be shown that the parts do not exist independently. This is determined through understanding. When one understands that all appearance (form) is mind, one abandons the conception of things. When one understands that the mind is a self-awareness, one abandons the conception of distinctions such as white, red, and so forth. When one's own self-awareness dawns as bliss, one abandons the conception of suffering and equanimity. When one realizes that bliss is without elaborations, one abandons attachment to that bliss. Thus, one understands the ultimate nature of the mind.

3. The Reasoning Refuting the Four Possibilities of Production
In one's meditation, one must avoid (a) four possible mis-

takes with regard to emptiness and (b) three other possible kinds of mistake.

(a) The four ways of misunderstanding emptiness

These are through mistaking the nature of emptiness (the object to be known), through misapplication, through mistaking the path, and through mistaking the antidote. The meditations in which these mistakes occur are practiced by persons who have not realized emptiness.[86]

Mistaking the nature of emptiness. For example, during meditation on the meaning of the *svabhāva shuddha* mantra, having conceptually arrived at an approximate idea of emptiness as being an utter negation, a person may then meditate on all existents as nonexistent. That person is mistaken through misunderstanding the nature of the object to be known — emptiness.

Misapplication. Someone may apply the term 'empty' to all things, thinking, 'This is empty; that also is empty.' This person is thereby establishing — as the object of his or her thought — a conception of general emptiness.[87] One does not thereby actually get at the real meaning of emptiness, however; emptiness is thus misunderstood through misapplication.

Mistaking the path. If a person does not understand that one attains the fruition through realizing that the fruit and the basis (the basic mode of abiding — emptiness) are inseparable, then he or she may expect to attain a good fruition by following a path. Such a person is mistaken with regard to the path.

Mistaking the antidote. A person may not realize that there is no difference between the object to be abandoned and its antidote and may therefore view friend and enemy as different.[88] Such a view generates desire and aversion, as well as the conceptions of subject and object; and these are the very things that must be abandoned.

(b) The three places of possible error

There are many who say that a meditation in which one experiences any of these three — bliss, clarity, and non-conceptuality — is a supreme meditation. However, these also can be sources of error in meditation, because: through attachment to bliss, one is reborn in the desire realm; through attachment to clarity, in the form realm; and through attachment to nonconceptuality, in the formless realm.

Even if you meditate without attachment to bliss, clarity, and nonconceptuality, if you do not realize emptiness, the highest fruit you can attain is the condition of high rebirth in the realms of gods and humans. Lord Jigten Sumgön says: "States of flawless meditative equipoise are the causes of rebirth in the three realms." However, if you meditate without falling into these errors, you will understand the very foundation of the mind.

4. The Reasoning of Dependent-Arising
This is the reasoning analyzing all phenomena, the fourth of the four ways of realizing that the mind of self-awareness is without true existence. In this regard, it is said that the antidotes to ignorance are the 12 branches of dependent-arising. Nāropa says:

> Being an awareness,
> The mind of self-awareness
> Has the nature of luminosity.
> Being nonconceptual,
> It does not conceive of itself.

The very nature of such a mind is nonconceptuality. Let us take, as an example, a person who has a mind of self-awareness which is an exalted wisdom. When that person realizes that the mind is exalted wisdom, it is said that he or she ceases to look elsewhere for Buddha. However, the mind of self-awareness can be obstructed by temporary stains. The mind afflicted by conceptuality is like water, gold, and space, in this way: in their relative states, all these are subject to distinctions of pure and impure, but their true nature is luminosity. In their true nature, even the slightest stain is utterly nonexistent.

Just as outer phenomena do not exist, so inner phenomena[89] do not exist; just as inner phenomena do not exist, so outer phenomena do not exist. It is said that sentient beings are not sentient beings; however, it is not the case that they do not exist. One must come to realize the ultimate nature free from the conventional nature.

Furthermore, all phenomena, from forms through omniscient consciousnesses, are dependent-arisings; dependent-arisings are momentary phenomena; momentary phenomena are produced from conditions; that which is produced from conditions is not produced inherently.

As the Buddha said:

> That which is produced from conditions is not
>   produced,
> Because it is without inherent production.
> That which depends on conditions is emptiness.
> One who knows emptiness is aware.

This is how one is to understand the true foundation of the mind. One who has such understanding is said to possess the realization that is not touched by the three great views.[90] There is no assertion.[91] As Lord Jigten Sumgön says:

> Finally, realize directly the Truth Body: such realization transcends the three great views; it is utterly free of viewing, object of view, and agent of view. This is a special feature of our system, not possessed by any other.
>   Those three great views are of course needed. But if you are not free from attachment to high status,[92] then you will not realize the view; you will not get at the real view.

The real view is free of assertion. As Lord Jigten Sumgön says:

> Since I have no assertion,
> I do not incur those faults.
> The Conqueror said nothing to his disciples;
> Then he explained extensively
> That which had been unsaid.

Thus, the view must be accompanied by realization. Having realized the view, meditate on it.

MEDITATION ON THE VIEW

In order to meditate on the view, you must practice the technique of body posture, the technique of time of practice, and the technique of stabilizing the mind. All are to be practiced together.

The Technique of Body Posture

The proper arrangement of your body, in the sevenfold Vairochana posture, will permit realization to appear to your mind. Buddha said in *The Diamond Rosary Sutra:*

> Sit on a comfortable cushion. Direct your eyes toward the tip of your nose. Your nose should be aligned with your navel; your shoulders, level; your tongue against the root of your mouth; your lips and teeth positioned comfortably. Then, having relaxed your breathing, breathe with only very slight effort, according to your teacher's instructions; remain in the proper cross-legged posture.

Practice well this technique of body posture.

The Technique of Time of Practice

The technique of time of practice is to practice at all times. It is said that there are no practice sessions as such.[93] Whenever there is mindfulness, the conqueror of time, there is meditation. All times are appropriate for practice.

There is no need to calculate the month and date; there is no need to take into account the positions of sun, moon, and stars; the time of practice is not limited in any way. You should practice continuously, without formal sessions.

The Technique of Stabilizing the Mind

The technique of stabilizing the mind has two parts, 1. meditation on the mode of abiding of phenomena and 2. identification of that mode of abiding. The first of these — the meditation — in turn has two stages. The stage of completion with signs involves holding one's mind at the drops in the five places in one's body. The stage of completion without signs involves the seven methods of mind stabilization.[94]

1. Meditation on the mode of abiding of phenomena

(a) Practicing the stage of completion with signs

When cultivating this part of the technique for stabilizing the mind, first generate a mind of enlightenment and then visualize your body as that of the yidam deity. Be mindful of the teacher as Vajradhara and then meditate by placing your mind without distraction at the luminous blue drop, the size of a mustard seed, at your heart. If a good meditative stabilization then arises, rest briefly in a relaxed natural state[95] without anything appearing to your mind.

Then, again set your mind one-pointedly on the drop at the heart. Keep your mind on that drop; if any thought should arise, pay no attention to it. Practice this way in four sessions daily. Finally, stop observing even the drop; then set your mind in the natural nonartificial state.[96]

If this practice causes excitement to arise in your mind, then meditate on the yellow drop at the navel and the green drop at the secret place of yourself as the yidam deity. If lethargy arises in your mind, meditate on the red drop at the throat and on the white drop at the forehead of the deity.

If you meditate in this way, your mind will not scatter

outward; it will remain in a nonconceptual state. Clairvoyance and other good qualities will then arise. As is said in the *Chakrasamvara Tantra:*

> By keeping the mind inside,
> One achieves whatever one wills.

(b) Practicing the stage of completion without signs

In this part of the technique of stabilizing the mind, there are seven methods:

(1) Sustaining the practice without taking anything to mind.
(2) Sustaining the practice while abandoning any conception of distinctions.
(3) Sustaining the practice without losing mindfulness.
(4) Sustaining the practice with great effort.
(5) Sustaining the practice in regard to the meaning of nonmeditation.
(6) Sustaining the practice without the extremes of tightness and looseness of mind.
(7) Sustaining the practice with one's mind in the natural state.

(1) Sustaining the practice without taking anything to mind. Nāgārjuna says:

> All phenomena are equally selfless. One's mind is, from the beginning, nonproduced and is of the nature of emptiness; that which is the very nature or essence of emptiness — the mind is that. The yogi meditating on the meaning of emptiness is neither breathing nor not breathing; his eyes are neither opened nor closed; his body is neither straight nor bent. He neither talks nor does not talk. He does not think about external objects; he does not think about his mind. There are eleven things that are not taken to mind: form, sound, smell, taste, and tangibility are not taken to mind; the nature of form,

sound, smell, taste, and tangibility are not taken to mind; and phenomena are not taken to mind.

When the Precious Lord Jigten Sumgön stayed with his family at Den in eastern Tibet, a neighboring wife's husband died, and she was very sad. The Precious Lord's mother said to her neighbor, "Cease to think about your husband, and your suffering will cease. If you continue to think about him, the pain will continue." Later, Jigten Sumgön came to central Tibet and met with the teacher Phagmo Drupa. Later still, after Jigten Sumgön had directly realized mahamudra, he felt that of all the teachings expressed by Phagmo Drupa, none was higher than this — of not taking anything to mind.

It follows that this teaching of not taking anything to mind is very profound. Saraha says:

> Not taking to mind —
> This is the body of mahamudra.
> Yogi, do not allow yourself to hope
> For any fruit whatsoever.

(2) Sustaining the practice while abandoning any conception of such distinctions as high and low and so forth. Do not meditate while conceiving of good, bad, and neutral. Tilopa said:

> If one does not think of good and bad,
> The thoughts of the Buddhas of
> The three times will dawn.
> All the omniscient ones teach this.

The three times are the past, present, and future. Tilopa also said:

> Abide in a natural state, completely without physical action; speak little; meditate on the emptiness of your voice, like an echo. Look at the mode of abiding of phenomena without anything appearing to mind.

Stabilize your mind on the mode of abiding of phenomena; this meditative stabilization, in which all confusions have been eliminated, is meditation without thought.

(3) Sustaining the practice without losing mindfulness. The Precious Lord Jigten Sumgön says:

> One must understand the importance of maintaining mindfulness; without mindfulness, there is no meditation and thus no method.

This firm mindfulness is very important. Mindfulness encompasses the 37 branches of enlightenment, which are: the four aspects of mindfulness, the four perfect abandonments, the four foundations of miraculous power, the five powers, the five controlling powers, the seven branches of enlightenment and the noble eightfold path.[97]

One who sustains this practice achieves all the levels of Never-Returner, of one who has achieved the union of no-more-learning. These high levels, and all the other levels below them, depend on mindfulness.

First one attains the *four aspects of mindfulness*. Then, through this — developing the entity of these four — one attains the *four perfect abandonments*. Continuing this development — stabilizing mindfulness more and more — one eliminates the objects of abandonment and thereby attains the *four foundations of miraculous power;* one of these is the stabilization of mindfulness. After these four stabilizations, the *five powers* are attained; one of them is the power of mindfulness.

The five powers are made stronger and stronger, until the *five controlling powers* are attained; one of them is the controlling power of mindfulness. The controlling powers are developed more and more, until the *seven branches of enlightenment* are attained; one of them is the perfection of mindfulness. The seven perfections are developed until the eight branches of the *eightfold path* are attained; one of these is right mindfulness.

Completion of the eightfold path is the completion of

practice: the state of a Learner is attained. This state is developed to perfection, and finally, through mindfulness, one is empowered by the peaceful meditative stabilization to attain the exalted wisdom of the stage of Never-Returner. Lord Jigten Sumgön says: "Familiarization with realization is meditation"; this is training without losing mindfulness.

(4) Sustaining the practice with great effort. Jigten Sumgön said:

> Great effort means
> Uninterrupted mindfulness;
> If you do not understand this,
> Your practice will suffer.

You should sustain your practice with a steadiness like the steady gait of an elephant or the steady tension of a guitar string. Tilopa said:

> One who cannot sustain this practice
> Should practice a technique of breath and remain in
>   the naked mind.[98]
> With the many methods of attaining the view and
>   holding the mind,
> Practice until your mind is stabilized.

This means that you are to stabilize your mindfulness, not allowing it to waver for even a moment. Without moving your eyes or blinking, set your mind in a nonconceptual meditative state.

(5) Sustaining the practice in regard to the meaning of nonmeditation. There is no object of observation of meditation and no place of meditation. Jigten Sumgön said:

> No object of meditation,
> Not the slightest trace;
> No flicker of attention,
> Not even for a moment —
> This is the heart-teaching of mahamudra.

He also said:

There is no meditation, but familiarization comes;
And as it becomes familiar, you will understand the
    view.
You alone can do this; set your mind steadily in
    meditative equipoise.

In the *Guhyasamāja Tantra* is written:

There is no meditation on a nonexistent thing;
The object of meditation is not meditated on.
Since neither things nor non-things exist,
There is no thing to observe in meditation.

(6) Sustaining the practice without the extremes of tightness and looseness. If your mind is tight, mental excitement arises, making impossible the virtuous activity of meditation. Such unfavorable conditions cause the mind to go out to external objects. Thus, do not overtighten your mind.

If it is held too loosely, your mind will wander unnoticed below the surface and you will not be aware of its movement. Thus, guard against the extremes of tightness and looseness. The practice of virtue should be like the balancing of a scale. Saraha said:

The mind that is bound tightly by thought
Will definitely be liberated
If it is loosened to just the right tension,
As a Brahmin spins his thread.
Keep your mind in a fresh, nonartificial, natural
    state.

(7) Sustaining the practice with one's mind in a natural, nonartificial state. The Buddha says in the *Prajñaparamita Sutra:*

Practice free of artifice
Causes supreme enlightenment;
The power of the artificial
Prevents attainment of the noble path.

Keep your mind in the fresh, natural state without artificially changing its true nature. If you meditate on something as existent, that is artificial. If you meditate on something as nonexistent, that also is artificial. If you meditate on something as being between the two extremes of existence and nonexistence, that also is artificial.

'Fresh' refers to the state beginning after the cessation of a conceptual thought and lasting until the arising of another conceptual thought.

'Natural' means you are to set your mind on the various objects appearing to the six consciousnesses, without accepting some and rejecting others.

'Nonartificial' means that whatever dawns in your self-luminous mind is to be sustained without your making any changes. This is taught in the text called *Seven Ways of Settling the Mind.* Learn to recognize the nonartificial consciousness, and keep your mind in a nonartificial state. Through understanding that the earlier and later moments of mind are one, your concentration will be ignited like a fire. This powerful state of concentration will generate a fruition of good qualities, limitless as space.

These seven methods of stabilizing the mind can all be included in the first of the seven: sustaining practice without taking anything to mind (also called meditation free from mental engagement). Lord Jigten Sumgön says:

> Not spoiled by the effort of good thought, not following after bad thought, and not going to the neutral — set your mind in meditation, free from mental engagement.

'Spoiled by the effort of good thought' means letting your meditation be spoiled by the effort of forming a concept, like 'suchness is emptiness; suchness is selflessness.' The Buddha says in the *Prajñaparamita Sutra:*

> A Bodhisattva who thinks 'this aggregate is empty' is engaged in conceptual designation and thus has no faith in the state of abiding without production.

'Following after bad thought' means that because of un-favorable conditions, one's thought goes out to external objects. In the *Pramāṇāvarttika* is written:

> If one conceives of 'self,' then one must also con-ceive of 'other.' Attachment and aversion arise as a result of these two conceptions — of self and other. As a result of relationships accompanied by feelings of attachment and aversion, all faults are generated. It should be understood that the root of all those faults is this view — that the transitory aggregation called I and mine has an inherent existence.

'Going to the neutral' means seeing faults in conceptual thought and seeing good qualities in nonconceptual thought; this too is to be avoided. Do not allow your mind to dwell on the characteristics of objects. Set your mind in meditative stabilization free from mental engagement.

The meaning of 'meditation free from mental engage-ment' is shown in Tilopa's summation of his work on maha-mudra:

> When attachment arises, the clear light of the basic
>   mind is obstructed and not seen.
> To keep the pledges conceptually is to fall away
>   from their true meaning.
> One's own birth and death are like waves on the
>   ocean.
> One who holds fast to the true meaning of
>   non-observation will keep the pledges.
> Realization of the true meaning — mahamudra — is
>   the light that illuminates the darkness.
> One who is free from all grasping is not drawn to
>   the extremes; such a one understands the
>   discourses.
> One who follows this true meaning will be liberated
>   from the prison of cyclic existence.
> Stabilize your mind in this meaning; all sins and
>   obstructions will be burned away.
> This is the Lamp of the Teachings.

'Meditation free from mental engagement' means stabilization of the mind on mahamudra. Mahamudra is the true
meaning of reality and the ultimate mode of abiding of
phenomena.

2. Identification of the mode of abiding of phenomena

The identification of the mode of abiding of phenomena has
two parts, identification of meditative equipoise as calm-
abiding and identification of self-awareness as mahamudra.

(a) Identification of meditative equipoise as calm-abiding

First, meditate without conceptions of past, present, and
future. Having fully subdued all conceptions of things and
names, remain in this state: one-pointed, without conception, unsullied by any of the three moods — laxity, excitement, and lethargy. This state is called 'calm-abiding' or
'meditative equipoise.'
  The glorious Shawari says of this state:

> The taste of nondual innate bliss
> Is like the taste of water mixed with water.
> Abiding in the true nature as it is —
> This is called fully subduing the mind
> That clings to objects.

  Calm-abiding is the basis for the generation of all good
qualities. As the Buddha said:

> If one cannot hold the mind one-pointed and
>   balanced,
> One does not have pure exalted wisdom,
> And cannot cast off the contaminations.

The teachings of the Buddha are not realized by other
paths. If one attains the great wisdom of calm-abiding, then
one definitely will be liberated. Furthermore, Shāntideva
says in *Engaging in the Bodhisattva Deeds*:

> Special insight joined with strong calm-abiding will
> annihilate completely the afflictions. Know this for

yourself. First, become skilled in calm-abiding; this you can do if you are not attached to worldly things and have a happy mind.

(b) Identification of self-awareness as mahamudra

Mahamudra is also known as 'pure nonconceptual special insight.' The Buddha said:

> O Son of the Noble Family, a Bodhisattva who has attained meditative stabilization is not satisfied with this mere calm-abiding and with the mere taste of meditative stabilization. Remaining in that meditative stabilization, he counts the phenomena of the great vehicle, analyzes the objects of comprehension, and investigates individually the teachings of the great vehicle. The conceptual thought that counts, analyzes, and investigates such phenomena, objects, and teachings will fully generate special insight.

THE QUINTESSENTIAL INSTRUCTIONS

After having generated the clear meditative equipoise of calm-abiding, and while remaining in that state, investigate the true nature of that mind of calm-abiding, using the very mind of calm-abiding itself. Investigate well, thinking, "Does it exist or not? Does it have color or not?"

If you think it exists, then investigate well, thinking: "How was it first generated? Where did it come from? Where does it remain? Where will it end?" If you think it does not exist, then investigate, thinking: "Who thinks it is nonexistent? Who superimposes 'nonexistent'?" If you think it is beyond existence and nonexistence, then investigate the way in which it is beyond them. Through practicing in this way, you can arrive at the foundation of the mind — mahamudra.

Lord Jigten Sumgön says: "When one sees that the mind flits from thing to thing, that — not seeing anything — is seeing." One's mind is, from the beginning, free from all extremes of existence and nonexistence, being and non-being, good and bad, permanence and annihilation, and so forth. The true nature of one's mind cannot be described in any way. The realization of that true nature of the mind is called mahamudra or 'the wisdom of self-awareness.'[99] In the *Prajñaparamita Sutra*, Buddha says:

> Sentient beings will say, for example, 'I see the sky'; however, if one investigates, it is difficult to explain what it means to see the sky. The Tathāgatas explained that this is what the sensing of phenomena is like; such seeing cannot be illustrated by anything else.

Tilopa says:

> For example, it has often been said that the sky is empty, but there is no way to describe how the sky is by saying 'it is like this' or 'it is like that.' Similarly, although one's mind is called luminous, there is no basis for describing it — no basis for saying 'the mind is established in such and such a way.' The nature of the mind is, from the beginning, like space. There is no phenomenon that is not included in that space-like nature, which is mahamudra. All phenomena, without exception, are included in the mind.

Such a realization — that your mind is, from the beginning, without production, abiding, and cessation — is called 'the ordinary mind,' 'the Nature Body,' and 'the self-arisen innate exalted wisdom.' Lord Gampopa says, "I sustain this ordinary mind." This entity (the ordinary mind) is the meditative stabilization of the Mahayana path of seeing.

From this point of view, all of your consciousnesses, which scatter to myriad objects, are not different from your basic mind; rather, your various consciousnesses and your basic mind are identified as one. This is to be known.

Lord Gampopa also says:

Mind is the innate Truth Body;
Form is the light of the innate Truth Body.
Thus, form and mind are inseparably united.

The Master Toktsepa says:

The ordinary mind is awakened in the center of the
heart.
If the six consciousnesses are pure, then bliss will
not cease.
All actions of body, speech, and mind are
purposeless;
Apart from being the cause of suffering, they are
without meaning.
Remain in the natural state without meditative
effort.

Lord Jigten Sumgön identifies view, meditation, and
activity in this way:

The view is the unmistaken realization of the meaning of the mind.[100] Meditation is keeping the mind
on that — the correct view, which is accompanied
by realization — without distraction.
    Virtuous activity is action that accords with this
meditation. It is true of all phenomena — in cyclic
existence and nirvana — that unless the appropriate causes and conditions exist, the phenomena will
not arise.
    Phenomena are merely dependent-arisings. De-
pendent-arisings abide only momentarily. The moments of their abiding are also dependent-arisings;
they are empty. Being empty, they are the Truth
Body, the fruition.

The six objects of consciousness appear dualistically as
cyclic existence and nirvana. Subject and object do not exist
separately, as two. Suppose you are looking one-pointedly

at something, a pillar or a pot, in front of you; the mind does not really follow the object. The object appears merely through a combination of dependent-arisings; that is all. Ultimately, there is no establishment as subject and object in regard to any phenomenon whatsoever. From the beginning, appearance and mind (object and subject) abide as a self-liberating unity.[101] As it is said in the *King of Meditative Stabilization Sutra:*

> See the moon rising in a clear sky:
> Its reflection appears in a clear lake,
> But the moon itself is not in the water.
> Understand all phenomena in this way.

Nāropa said:

> The nature of appearance is without production;
> And the nature of cyclic existence is without
>   foundation.
> The nature of the mind is the unity of appearance
>   and emptiness.

You must understand that appearance and mind are simply a unity; and you must understand that conceptual thought is itself the basic mind. Saraha said:

> Whatever elaborations arise from the mind,
> These are the nature of the Truth Body.
> Are the water and the waves different?
> No, they are equally like the sky.

Lord Jigten Sumgön said:

> The Truth Body, which is the ultimate fruition,
> Is none other than the afflictions.
> Wisdom and ignorance are not two, but one.
> Ignorance is the great wisdom.

He also said:

> Products are without production, like space.
> Nonproducts are without production, like space.

The Truth Body is without production, like space.

Practice is sustained through appearance itself, through neither accepting nor rejecting what appears. Whatever appears, whatever you see, that itself is empty; emptiness is not something apart from the ordinary phenomena that appear to you. These are the quintessential instructions.

PRACTICING IN ACCORDANCE WITH THE QUINTESSENTIAL INSTRUCTIONS

If you practice in accordance with the quintessential instructions, the unity of dependent-arising and emptiness dawns as cause and effect. Then, emptiness dawns as cause and effect.[102] Therefore, you must train in the special behavior of Superiors, the precious ethics.

Furthermore, in this system of teachings, the view includes realization, meditation is free from mental engagement, and action is free from accepting and rejecting. Lord Jigten Sumgön says:

> The precious lama (Lord Phagmo Drupa) understood that all migrators wander in cyclic existence because they hold a view of the aggregates as inherently existent — a view that is false because of mental elaborations. Therefore, the lama taught the view free from elaboration; he taught meditation on that view without distraction; and he taught practice of the ethics of the Buddha. These three — pure view, pure meditation, and pure practice — are the supreme essence of the Buddha's teaching.
>
> This supreme essence does not flourish today except in the teachings of the precious lama. I have thought deeply about how this teaching is to be spread, and as a result of my deep wish I received all the teachings from Phagmo Drupa. Then I knew it would be possible for the teaching of the excellent lama to continue without interruption.

Engaging in the pure practice of ethics, one does not adopt sin and one does not reject virtue; in this way the eye of cause and effect is found. Practicing the correct acceptance and rejection, one will attain the fruit in this very life. The Precious Lord Jigten Sumgön says:

> Mahamudra is simply this self-awareness. Sustaining this practice without distraction is cultivation of the fundamental Truth Body.[103] That which brings about enhancement of mahamudra is devotion to the excellent lama. To understand every appearance whatsoever as the Truth Body is to understand mahamudra. To realize conceptuality as the Truth Body is to realize mahamudra. The happiness that arises both in cyclic existence and beyond it is the quality of mahamudra. The benefiting of beings by the Four Bodies is the activity of mahamudra.

The four bodies, the eight signs, the eight common feats, and so forth, will be achieved through the practice of mahamudra. One's attainment of such fruition depends on the coming together of the necessary causes and conditions. This is because, as the Buddha said: "All phenomena follow after causes, depend on conditions, and depend on one's aspiration."

CONCLUDING PRACTICES
Dedication

Dedication

One needs to aspire strongly and to perform dedication.
Lord Gampopa says:

> I am not one who has not accumulated virtue; but
> my virtue is wasted, simply because I do not under-
> stand the method of dedication.

And the Buddha said in the *Prajñaparamita Sutra:*

> After arising from that meditative session, perform
> faultless virtuous practices, then dedicate the merit
> of your practices to the attainment of highest en-
> lightenment for sentient beings. If you perform this
> dedication, there is no virtue in the three realms to
> equal it.

One must perform the dedication. Lord Jigten Sumgön
says:

> If the wish-fulfilling jewel of the two accumulations
> Is not polished by your aspiration,
> Your goal will not be reached;
> Attend, therefore, to this final dedication.

THE DAKORMA DEDICATION[104]

Visualize in the space in front of you a pure field with the lions, precious throne, and so forth; on top of these are the lama and yidam deities, Buddhas and Boddhisattvas, and Dakas, Dakinis, and Dharma-Protectors.

Cultivate well the pure motivation, the generation of the altruistic mind. Call to mind the objects of observation — the virtues accumulated in the three times and the innate root of virtue (the Buddha nature, *Tathāgatagarbha*) of all sentient beings — and then dedicate all of these to the attainment of highest enlightenment for all sentient beings.[105]

The Suitability of Dedicating Innate Virtue

There are some who argue that it is not suitable to dedicate the innate virtue. However, the suitability of that dedication can be shown in three ways: by the Buddha's word, by reasoning, and by the quintessential instructions.

1. The Buddha's word on dedication of the innate virtue. The Buddha said: "The dedication without object of observation — that is the unsurpassed dedication."[106] He also said:

> Dedication in which there is conceptuality (the conception of the three spheres of agent, action, and object) is not the supramundane dedication. Dedication in which there is no conceptuality is supramundane dedication. Making a dedication with conceptuality is like eating good food mixed with poison. The good food represents virtue, poison the conception of the three spheres. Observing phenomena — even virtuous phenomena — is like eating food mixed with poison.

In the *Medicine Deity Sutra,* the Buddha said, "By the power of the very pure inconceivable sphere of reality,[107] may what I wish for come to pass; may all sentient beings be established in Buddhahood."[108] He also spoke of "the innate root of virtue, which is the unsurpassable wisdom." In all of these statements, the Buddha was referring to the innate virtue.

2. Reasoning on dedication of the innate virtue. There are some who raise the objection, "If the innate virtue changes (is the cause of an effect), it follows logically that suchness is a caused phenomenon. If the innate virtue does not change, it can not produce an effect; and so the dedication of it is meaningless. If the dedication of innate virtue could produce an effect, why is the act of dedication of the first Buddha not bearing fruit now?"

In response, it can be argued, "If dedication of a noncreated object has no effect, then, if one expresses the power of the truth of suchness, that truth will become powerless (will be unable to produce an effect) because it is a nonproduct."

3. Quintessential instructions on dedication of the innate virtue. Many precious Lamas have given instructions on how to perform the dedication of the innate virtue.

The Objects to be Dedicated
The objects to be dedicated are the many virtues you have accumulated in the three times and the innate virtue, your own Buddha nature.

The Recipients of the Dedication
These virtues are to be dedicated to all the innumerable sentient beings, throughout all of space. The Buddha said:

> Just as the sky is without limit,
> So is the number of sentient beings;
> Just as their actions and afflictions are without
>   limit,
> So are my wishes for their welfare.

The Purpose of the Dedication
The eight worldly concerns and the four causes of cyclic existence[109] are not the objects to be attained. The fruitional

state of the Hearer and Solitary Realizer states is the Foe Destroyer (*Arhaṭ*) state, but even this is not the object to be attained. Do not stay on the level of Foe Destroyer. That which is to be attained is the rank of the great Vajradhara, the state of the union of emptiness and bliss.

Perform the dedication, therefore, together with the exalted wisdom that is completely free of the three spheres.[110] One who is free of the three spheres knows the emptiness of all phenomena, is without conceptuality, and has no wish for fruit. These freedoms are to be conjoined with the exalted wisdom without object of observation. This is expressed in this way in the dedication chapter of *The Diamond Banner:*

> By my dedicating the innate virtue of all sentient beings and the accumulated virtue of the deeds of all sentient beings in the past, present, and future, may all sentient beings attain Buddhahood.

In performing the dedication, visualize the objects of refuge, which are to be the witnesses of your dedication. Think that they are in front of you, all united in seeking the fulfilment of your dedication. Then say the *dakorma* dedication prayer:

> I dedicate the innate virtue of myself and all sentient beings, as well as the accumulated virtues — those accumulated by us in mundane and supramundane realms, in cyclic existence, and in nirvana. By the power of these, may I and all sentient beings quickly attain the precious rank of Buddhahood.

By performing this dedication, you will attain the ornament wheel[111] of inexhaustible fruition (Buddhahood); and your attainment will be irreversible. The Buddha says of dedication:

> Then, with the mandala in front of you, sit with your hands together at your heart; observe all sen-

tient beings and pray with a compassion that is without object of observation.

Maitreya said in the *Abhisamayālaṃkāra:*

That supreme dedication,
Without object of observation —
That is the supreme deed,
That is the unmistaken dedication.

Establish the essence of the fruit by this dedication.

Colophon

SVASTI   This clarification of the stages of the path — of ripening empowerments and liberating teachings — flows from the sutras and tantras, from the commentaries, and from the quintessential instructions. By traversing these stages, one acquires the nondualistic wisdom of the vajra mind, which completely removes the veils — the two obstructions.

May I attain the supreme path in this lifetime.
May I attain the rank of Vajradhara, Lord of
   Conquerors, excellent lama possessing the Four
   Bodies:
The glorious innate Exalted Wisdom Body, the
   union of emptiness and compassion;
The Complete Enjoyment Body and the Emanation
   Body, which appear to sentient beings
   spontaneously and effortlessly;
And the Fourth Body, fulfilling the two purposes
   — of oneself and others.
Having attained this supreme state, may I bring to
   fruition all sentient beings without exception.

Here, in *Clarifying the Jewel Rosary of the Profound Five-*

fold Path, I have set forth the pure meaning, without deviating from the pure view and without embellishment, in accordance with the thought of the glorious Phagmo Drupa, precious lord of all sentient beings; of Jigten Sumgön, precious lord of dharma, omniscient and without equal; and of their spiritual sons.

This work clears away nonunderstanding, mistaken understanding, and doubts. It was written for those who are interested in living in accordance with the teachings of those who maintain our Kagyu system, so that they may realize the meaning of the teachings. I, Kunga Ratna Chökyi Gyaltsen Pal Sangpo, have written this to help the spread and increase of the treasure, the teachings of the Conqueror Drikungpa, and because Shampa Lama of Yarlung and others asked me to. This work was written in the Pema Sambhava place of meditation at White Rock on the first day of the fifth month in the year of the female watersheep. It is now completed.

MANGALAM BAVANTU SHUBHAM

APPENDIX:
The Life Story of the Author, Kunga Rinchen

The second Victorious One, Gyalwang Kunga Pal Sangpo (1475-1527) was the fifteenth successor of Lord Jigten Sumgön, and in fact was Lord Jigten Sumgön himself, reincarnated for the purpose of revivifying the teachings of the Buddha in a time when they had declined. Kunga Rinchen was born in Dru Trashi Teng Palace in the wood-sheep year. His father was Chökyi Je Rinchen Chökyi Gyaltsen and his mother was Rinchen Palmo. At the time of his birth the earth trembled, rainbows appeared, a rain of flowers fell from the sky, and a five-colored bridge of light radiated from the image of Lord Jigten Sumgön at Changchub Ling monastery to the place where the child, named Rinchen Lhunpo, was born.

During his childhood, Kunga Rinchen played at building monasteries, temples, and stupas and at giving teachings to other children. He also recited the *Mañjushri-namasaṃgiti*. At the age of seven he was taught to read and write by his teacher, Jyin Drak. Kunga Rinchen was ten when his father died. He tried to comfort his mother, telling her not to be distressed and advising her as to the proper ceremonies and observances. Soon after this, Kunga Rinchen fell ill and had a vision of the Medicine Buddha, who appeared in the sky and radiated light, which cured his illness.

Kunga Rinchen received instruction on the essence of the Mahayana teachings and many other topics from Karmapa Chödrak Gyatso (the seventh Karmapa), who recognized him as the reincarnation of Lord Jigten Sumgön. From Dharma Lord Wang Rinpochay, Kunga Rinchen received all the written and oral teachings of Lord Jigten Sumgön. He worked hard in his studies, hearing these teachings, thinking well about their meaning, and meditating one-pointedly on their essence. In particular, he achieved the final realization of the four yoga stages of the practice of the fivefold profound path of mahamudra.

At the time of this realization, Kunga Rinchen had a dream in which pus and blood came out of his body. He reported it to his teacher, Wang Rinpochay, who said, "This is a sign that you have completely purified your karmic obscurations, obstacles to liberation, and obstacles to omniscience."

At the age of 17, Kunga Rinchen took the vows of a novice monk from Khenchen (Great Abbot) Kunga Lodrö; from the Lobpön (Master) Lodrö Tenpa; from Lekba Rinchen, who determined the proper time for his taking the vows; and from others. He took the name Kunga Rinchen Chökyi Gyaltsen Pal Sangpo.

As a novice, Kunga Rinchen received many empowerments and instructions from his abbot, Kunga Lodrö. Under the Lopbön Lodrö Tenpa he studied the *Root Sutra on the Discipline (Vinaya)* and other topics. He in turn pleased his teachers with many gifts. He studied the teachings of the six yogas of Nāropa under Jamyang Palden Rinchen and achieved the meditative stabilization of the great bliss of *tummo*, subsequently receiving a vision of the assembly of the peaceful and wrathful deities. He also studied the sutras and tantras under many other teachers.

At the age of 20, in the wood-tiger year, Kunga Rinchen became a fully ordained monk (*bhikṣhu*), in the presence of the abbot and other teachers. In that same year he was enthroned on the lion throne of Lord Jigten Sumgön; the event was marked by the appearance of many marvelous signs.

Because of many circumstances, the teachings of Lord Jigten Sumgön had been in decline in the years before Kunga Rinchen's enthronement, with only their essence remaining. With the fearless lion's roar of the teaching in the community of monks, he turned the wheel of the vast and profound teachings of Lord Jigten Sumgön and his disciples. In the winter he gave the teaching of the six yogas of Nāropa, and at Layel in Drikung he and hundreds of his disciples, clad only in thin cotton garments, displayed the heat of *tummo*. The frozen rivers in that area melted, the weather became summerlike, and rainbows and many other wonderful signs appeared. People from all over Tibet brought offerings, and in order to use them to bring about the greatest benefit, he gathered many copyists and had them copy the entire Kagyur twice and the entire Tangyur once on blue paper with gold and silver inks. With a number of other monks, he performed the blessing and consecration of these texts, then pleased the copyists with many gifts.

Inspired by the teaching and example of Kunga Rinchen, hundreds of practitioners promised to go into retreat for three years, and some for life. He had many retreat houses built in the upper and lower parts of Changchub Ling and appointed the Lord of Attainments Drikung Rechen Rinchen Gyatso as retreat master. The great scholar Tsul Trim Gyatson was appointed to teach and supervise sadhanas, mandala construction, chanting, and philosophical studies. Kunga Rinchen initiated the study of the *Gong Chik* of Lord Jigten Sumgön at the philosophy college in lower Changchub Ling. Thousands of monks came from all over

Tibet to Changchub Ling to study and practice.

During the reign of King Rinpungpa Donyod Dorje, central Tibet was struck by a plague and a drought in the same year. The King came to Kunga Rinchen and asked him to do something to stop the suffering caused by these two disasters. His mastery of dependent-arising and of the power of blessing enabled Kunga Rinchen to alleviate the suffering and establish all in a better life.

Throughout his life, Kunga Rinchen was blessed by visions and signs indicating his high realization and his great ability to benefit sentient beings. Once, when he was visiting the Jokhang in Lhasa, light radiated from the heart of the statue of Shakyamuni Buddha and melted into Kunga Rinchen's heart. At Changchub Ling he had a vision of Vajradhara, Tilopa, Nāropa, Marpa, Milarepa, Gampopa, and Phagmo Drupa. In this vision Gampopa gave him a handful of pearls, saying "These are your disciples." The meaning of this was that all his disciples would be of pure mind and able to greatly benefit sentient beings.

One winter Kunga Rinchen saw in a dream many butter lamps filling the area of Drikung. When he lit one, they all began to burn brightly. This was a sign that all his disciples would achieve great skill in *tummo*. Another night he dreamed he wore a stainless dharma robe and visited a huge plain with many flowers, some blossoming, others ready to blossom. This was a sign that his disciples were achieving the qualities of realization. When Kunga Rinchen gave teachings, Dakas and Dakinis came in the form of birds to hear them.

The activities of Kunga Rinchen extended beyond the immediate area of Drikung. He sent disciples to meditate at the holy mountains — Kailas, Lachi, and Tsari — where Milarepa, Gampopa, Lord Jigten Sumgön, and other great practitioners had sent their disciples in the past. To organize and administer such projects as building and maintaining monasteries, he appointed Gonbo Gyaltsen, an emanation of Mahakala.

Kunga Rinchen met with the fourth Shamarpa Rinpochay and exchanged offerings and teachings. On another occasion, a yogi, an emanation of Padmasambhava, came to Kunga Rinchen, gave him Nyingma teachings, and then disappeared.

One morning, during his first meditation of the day, Kunga Rinchen was visited by the wealth protector of Samye monastery, who told him that Samye had recently been restored and invited him to come to perform the consecration. Kunga Rinchen replied that he could not come, but would perform the consecration from where he was; and through his meditative powers he did so. At another time, Drikung came under attack by the jealous people of another region, but — thanks to the resistance of the local people and the aid of the Dharma Protectors — the attack was turned away.

At the age of 45, Kunga Rinchen accepted invitations to visit Dechen, Yangbachen, Lung, Dang, Chonggye, Trarong, and many other places, giving teachings and empowerments according to the needs of those who requested them, and establishing them on the path of enlightenment.

In his late forties, Kunga Rinchen commissioned the building of a stupa, Trashi Gomang ("many auspicious doors"), putting in charge of it the artisan Dorje Gyaltsen, a Bodhisattva emanation. This stupa was of six levels, adorned with many precious jewels, and it contained more than 3,200 images of lamas, yidam deities, Buddhas, Bodhisattvas, and Dharma Protectors. In accordance with the teaching of the higher tantric texts, Kunga Rinchen performed the blessing and consecration of the stupa with 50 other monks; he then rewarded the artisans with gifts that even Vaishravana could not have exceeded. All the local people took part in the celebration with singing, dancing, and music, and there were rainbows, rains of flowers, and many other auspicious signs.

At 50, Kunga Rinchen went to Terdrom for a retreat. There he had a vision of Guru Rinpochay (Padmasambhava) radiating the five colors, holding a hook and rope. Guru Rinpochay gave Kunga Rinchen a rosary with a number of beads equal to the number of years in his life. After Kunga Rinchen prayed again, Guru Rinpochay appeared again, this time in a palace of light and with his consort. On his way back to Drikung, Kunga Rinchen bathed in a lake, which turned to saffron color, while the whole area became filled with the scent of incense. He realized that this was an offering to him from the Dakinis.

Some time after this his mind turned to going to the Buddha fields, and during that summer and winter he gave teachings unreservedly, holding nothing back. To his disciple, Gyalwang Ratna, to the abbot, to the Lobpön, to the disciplinarian of Drikung, and to many other disciples he gave the essential teachings and the quintessential instructions, as well as teachings on impermanence and renunciation. He emphasized that the essence of the Buddha's teaching is practice. The motivation of his disciples shifted from the enjoyment of this life to the use of it to achieve highest enlightenment, and simultaneously their devotion increased.

Gradually, without any pain or sickness, Kunga Rinchen's body weakened and his desire for food decreased. While bathing, he would gaze at the sky and chant the six-syllable mantra of Chenresig and other dharma-songs. He travelled to Tseu Kha, and his weakness increased because he ate so little. He continued to meditate according to his regular schedule. He advised Gönbo Gyaltsen to build as soon as possible 12 statues of sandalwood representing the 12 events in the life of the Buddha, to repair the roof of the Serkhang temple where the statue of Lord Jigten Sumgön was kept, to make a lotus seat for that image, and in general to complete any projects that had been started.

Kunga Rinchen died at the age of 53, in the morning of the 26th day of the ninth month of the fire-pig year. In the area there appeared a rain of flowers, five-colored rainbows in all directions, and such other marvelous signs as many beings — some without form and some in the forms of rabbits and so forth — coming and performing prostration and circumambulation.

His highly realized disciples saw the Dharma Lord Kunga Rinchen himself going up among the rainbows in the sky and the Dakas and Dakinis making offerings to him. Many hundreds of monks performed offering rites in dependence upon the mandalas of the deities of the oceans of tantras. The Drikung monastery sent offerings to all the other monasteries throughout Tibet, without distinction as to order or lineage. A memorial shrine was built at Mount Kailas, and offerings were made to the three sacred mountains — Kailas, Lachi, and Tsari. Kunga Rinchen's body was placed in a silver stupa adorned with many jewels. After his death many wonderful manifestations, such as a conch shell spiralling to the right and special precious pills, appeared. In these many ways Gyalwang Kunga Rinchen caused the Buddha's teachings to flourish, and he produced many great disciples.

Those who wish to know more about Gyalwang Kunga Rinchen, his disciples, his teachings, and the very precious texts composed by him should consult *The Golden Rosary, the Lineage Record of the Protector, the Great Drikung Kagyu.*

Notes

1. His full name, as it appears in the colophon of *Clarifying the Jewel Rosary of the Profound Fivefold Path*, is Kunga Ratna Chökyi Gyaltsen Pal Sangpo. He is usually referred to as Gyalwang Kunga Rinchen, or simply as Kunga Rinchen.

2. The three wheels of doctrine are: teachings on the four noble truths, teachings about emptiness, and teachings on the definitive meaning (ultimate teachings about the unity of appearance and emptiness).

3. For a brief biography of Lord Jigten Sumgön, as well as some of his teachings, see *Prayer Flags: The Life and Spiritual Teachings of Jigten Sumgön*, translated by Ven. Khenpo Könchog Gyaltsen (Ithaca: Snow Lion Publications, 1986).

4. The three terms — teacher, guru (Sanskrit), and lama (Tibetan) — are used interchangeably in this work.

5. The Fourth Body, which is the 'composite in one of the Three Bodies,' is the Nature Body (*Svabhāvikakāya*) of a Buddha. The Three Bodies mentioned here are the Truth Body (*Dharmakāya*), the Complete Enjoyment Body (*Saṃbhogakāya*), and the Emanation Body (*Nirmāṇakāya*).

Later in the text (page 102) the author lists the Four Bodies as the Wisdom Body (*Jñānakāya*), the Complete Enjoyment Body, the Emanation Body, and the fourth, the Nature Body.

Generally, the Truth Body is named in a twofold division of Buddha Bodies into Truth Body and Form Body (*Rūpakāya*).

111

Each of these is then considered to have two parts: the Truth Body is composed of the Nature Body and the Wisdom Body; the Form Body is composed of the Complete Enjoyment Body and the Emanation Body. The Truth and Form Bodies are acquired through the completion of the accumulations of wisdom and merit respectively: see note 60.

6. All teachings of Lord Jigten Sumgön are based on the four validities: the words of the Buddha, the quintessential teachings of the great teachers, the true experiences of yogis, and the events in the lives of earlier great teachers.

7. The three streams of lineage are: the lineage of profound view, from Nāgārjuna; the lineage of profound action, from Asaṅga; and the lineage of blesssing meditation, from Tilopa.

8. The seven vajra topics are: Buddha, dharma (doctrine), sangha (assembly of Superiors), Buddha nature (essential wisdom element), enlightenment, perfect qualities of a Buddha, and activities of a Buddha.

9. Our attention to the teachings of the lama and to the four contemplations leads us to take refuge from the sufferings of cyclic existence in the Three Jewels (the Buddha, the dharma, and the sangha). After that decision, the four practices and the five meditations are the very life of the path.

10. These four contemplations have been briefly stated as 'impermanence, the precious human body, the faults of samsara, and karmic result.' In other words, worldly existence is full of suffering: the practice of virtue leads to the ending of suffering — liberation; to practice virtue we need a human body; and we have this body right now — but it will not last, it is impermanent.

11. These teachings are the four contemplations or antidotes or ways of turning the mind. The mistaken paths are our innumerable efforts to become comfortable in samsara.

12. The Vajrasattva practice is a specialized purification, which clears away ignorance and obstacles to omniscience as a mirror is cleared of dust. Through such purification, the basic mind, which is the Buddha nature, is revealed.

13. The two collections that must be completed if Buddhahood is to be attained are those of merit (virtue) and of wisdom. The idea 'the collections of the path' is also expressed as 'the accumulations of compassion and wisdom.'

In meditation we establish the mandala — symbol of the universe (all things, all sentient beings, ourselves, and our collections of virtue) — and then offer the mandala to the enlightened beings, giving it all away. This mental gesture of inward releasing helps to reduce our attachment to life; it genuinely helps us in realizing mahamudra — enlightenment.

14. Guru yoga brings blessings in the following way. If we see our teacher as an ordinary human being, we keep our minds in an ordinary state. If we practice guru yoga — deliberately thinking of the teacher as the root guru, Vajradhara — then our minds will tend toward the Vajradhara state, which itself is a blessing. When we really study and practice, a little bit of experience appears to the mind — a joyful, confident experience of nonartificial devotion. This is one of the most important Vajrayana practices. Through this devotion, one's doubts and hesitations are clarified. This is called the guru's blessing; it is the coming together of the teacher's compassion and wisdom, the teaching (which itself is a blessing), and one's own interest, devotion, and confidence.

15. See page 79 for a brief description of the sevenfold posture.

16. Temporary goodness is of two types, corresponding to rebirth in a human body or in the realm of gods; definite goodness is nirvana — no further rebirth.

17. The ten nonvirtues are: three nonvirtues of body: killing, stealing, and sexual misconduct; four of speech: lying, divisive talk, harsh speech, and foolish talk; three of mind: covetousness, harmful intent, and wrong views.

18. In this text, the instruction to visualize an 'excellent throne' or 'perfect seat' is a brief way of indicating that one is to visualize as support for the visualized lama or deity a throne held up by eight lions, a lotus, and the sun and moon discs.

19. The seven branches of offering are listed on page 62.

20. The ten directions include the four cardinal directions and the four intermediate directions, as well as the directions up and down.

21. The highest level of tantric practice, Highest Yoga Tantra, is divided into two stages: of generation and completion.

22. To set your mind in the mahamudra state means to realize mahamudra — emptiness. At that time, your mind is without thought, in a state which is beyond duality and non-duality.

23. *Hūṃ* (pronounced "hoong") is the seed syllable of Vajrasattva; the elements of the visualization all emerge from and then

return to the syllable *hūṃ*.

24. There are two types of obstructions: the obstructions to liberation are the afflictions of desire, hatred, and ignorance; the obstructions to omniscience are defined by Maitreya in his *Uttaratantra of the Great Vehicle* as the preconception of the three spheres — that is, the conception of inherently existent action, agent, and object. (These 'three spheres' are different from the 'three realms' described in note 40.)

25. This mantra is presented in accordance with Tibetan pronunciation; the standard Sanskrit transliteration is as follows:

Oṃ Vajrasattva, samayam anupālaya, Vajrasattva, tvenopatiṣṭha, dṛḍho me bhava, sutoṣhyo me bhava, supoṣhyo me bhava, anurakto me bhava, sarva-siddiṃ me prayachha, sarva-karmasu cha me chittaṃ shriyaṃ kuru, hūṃ ha ha ha ha hoḥ, bhagavan-sarva-tathāgata-vajra, mā me muñcha, vajrī bhava, mahāsamaya-satva, āḥ hūṃ phaṭ.

26. Actual accomplishments (*siddhi*) — powers and realizations acquired through spiritual practice — are of two types, ordinary and special. Ordinary accomplishments are those that one can attain without having reached the Mahayana path of seeing. Special accomplishments can only be attained by those who have reached that path. Enlightenment is sometimes described as the ultimate actual accomplishment.

27. The 'ornament' held in one's right hand consists of small pieces of precious stones and metals — such as turquoise, coral, gold, silver — mixed with grains of rice.

28. See note 18.

29. In this text, the terms 'root of virtue,' 'innate virtue,' and 'innate root of virtue' all refer to the Buddha nature.

30. The outer, inner, and secret offerings are discussed on page 62.

31. 'Actual accomplishment' here refers to enlightenment.

32. The 'two benefits': one's own enlightenment and the enlightenment of all sentient beings.

33. In the four brief meditation-prayers on pages 36 and 37, we visualize ourselves as one with the guru in order to purify our body, speech, mind, and wisdom.

The physical body must be purified before it can become for us the body of an enlightened deity. The 'obstruction of the waking state' is our thought that all phenomena are ordinary. By thinking instead of all phenomena as the enlightened state, we can transform the ordinary state of body and mind into the enlightened state.

Through purification of our speech we are empowered to recite the mantras. This power is a real but intangible quality akin to the power in a great artist's performance of a piece of music. Even before we achieve it, however, recitation of the mantras has good qualities.

The third prayer purifies our mental obscurations. Taking empowerment from the heart, we grow more able to practice compassion and wisdom.

The precious word empowerment enables us to practice non-duality — to realize the inseparability of the relative and the absolute states. The image is the state of changing, transformed into unchanging joy.

34. The great Vajradhara with the three bodies (page 68) is himself the Fourth Body, composite of the Three Bodies in one (page 21). He possesses the Four Bodies (page 102), and his rank is the state of the union of emptiness and bliss (page 100). This is the fourfold vajra state.

35. The 'blessing lineage' is the lineage descended from Tilopa. In this lineage, the student realizes mahamudra in himself or herself through strong devotion. Strong devotion produces a strong connection with the root guru, Vajradhara, and brings great blessings, which enable one to realize mahamudra.

36. Love is a gentle mind wishing that all sentient beings may have happiness. Compassion is a gentle, profound mind wishing that all sentient beings be free from suffering. Bodhichitta, a deep, spontaneous cherishing of others, is the aspiration to enlightenment in order to liberate all sentient beings from cyclic existence.

37. Champetop means 'power of love.' The Buddha's parable recounts the king's sacrificial offering of his own flesh and blood, rather than taking the lives of other beings.

38. The lower vehicle is the Hinayana vehicle, the higher is the Mahayana.

39. The tenth Bodhisattva ground *(bhūmi)* is Buddhahood.

40. There are three realms in cyclic existence: the desire realm *(kāmadhātu)*, the form realm *(rūpadhātu)*, and the formless realm *(ārūpyadhātu)*. Within the desire realm there are six categories of

migrators: gods, demigods, human beings, animals, hungry ghosts, and hell beings. The 'three lower realms' here refer to the last three of these six categories.

41. The three ethics are listed on page 61, see the index for other references.

42. The tantras of the category of Highest Yoga Tantra are of three types: mother, father, and nondual. The Chakrasamvara Tantra, one of many mother tantras, is used in the practice of mahamudra, because Chakrasamvara is the deity traditionally associated with mahamudra practice. Chakrasamvara is the yidam — the personal deity, the deity visualized by the meditator in the practice of deity yoga. This yidam practice (deity yoga) is very important because it can transform the ordinary state of mind into the enlightened state. In meditation one becomes the yidam deity in order to recognize the deity nature (which is the Buddha nature) in oneself. This is the secret of tantra.

43. The yoga of subtle drops, the four bodies, the eight signs, the channels and winds — these belong to yoga with signs. Beyond these are other practices, called yoga without signs. Practice of the stage of completion without signs is discussed on pages 81-88.

Deity yoga purifies the channels and winds of the body, helping to increase the capacity and creativity of the mind. This helps in the realization of mahamudra.

44. In properly following the practice, one is practicing the five perfections, and in doing that properly one is generating the five wisdoms; we purify ourselves to reveal them. Like the basic mind, they are already there within us and need only to be revealed.

45. The 'element of qualities' (*dharmadhātu*) or 'sphere of reality' is synonymous with emptiness, mahamudra.

46. The stage of generation is realizing (generating) oneself as a deity, step by step, from within emptiness (that is, with one's consciousness realizing emptiness). First, when one says the mantra, all phenomena are in a state of pervasive emptiness. Within the emptiness arise all the stages of the generation process, including the five perfections, until one realizes oneself completely as the yidam. One practices the meditation of the stage of generation — repeating the mantra, invoking the Buddha qualities of wisdom and compassion, and so forth. Then one practices the

stage of completion.

We must first understand what is emptiness and what is phenomenon, and then when we practice we realize their inseparable nature. This practice is also called a union of method and wisdom, because the consciousness realizing emptiness is also manifesting as the deity.

47. The standard Sanskrit transliteration is: *Oṃ svabhāva shuddha sarva dharma svabhāva shuddho haṃ.*

48. Heruka is another name for Chakrasamvara.

49. Heruka wears six ornaments, symbolizing the completion of the six perfections: giving, ethics, patience, effort, concentration, and wisdom. Vajrayogini wears five (see page 52), symbolizing the completion of the five perfections (see page 50).

50. See note 49.

51. The pledge-being is the visualized deity and is one of myriad wisdom-beings.

52. The five Buddha lineages or families are: Vajra, Jewel, Lotus, Activity, and Tathāgata.

53. That the three seats are completed means that one's body has been transformed into these three: five Buddha lineages, twelve Bodhisattvas, eight wrathful deities.

54. The standard Sanskrit transliteration of these four mantras is as follows:

Heruka essence: *Oṃ śrī vajra he he ru ru kam hūṃ hūṃ phaṭ; ḍākini jwala sambaram svāhā*

Heruka inner essence: *Oṃ hrīh ha ha hūṃ hūṃ phaṭ*

Vajrayogini essence: *Oṃ om om sarva Buddha ḍakinīye; vajra varnanīye; vajra vairochanīye; hūṃ hūṃ hūṃ phaṭ phaṭ phaṭ svāhā*

Vajrayogini inner essence: *Oṃ vajra vairochanī hūṃ phaṭ*

55. What is 'thoroughly established' is mahamudra, the unity of emptiness and appearance. It can be said that the relative itself is absolute, and the absolute itself is relative; for us it is a matter of realizing it, of experiencing it. This is why Kunga Rinchen says that the stage of generation is not imaginary: if it were, the qualities and powers of the Buddha nature could not be achieved — and they can be. We have basically all the Buddha qualities, but to reveal them, realize them, we do this practice.

56. Literally, diamond (*vajra*)-pride; sometimes described as 'divine pride' — one is completely identified with the body and mind of the deity appearing to one's mind.

57. These three mental practices are really just one practice described in three parts:

1) Meditation on clear form is essentially the clear visualization of oneself as a deity.

2) In 'mindfulness of the purity of the form,' 'purity' refers to the enlightened state, the pure state, the deity state. One is transforming the ordinary state into the enlightened pure state; this has two parts: a) mindfulness of the purity of the natural signs is the realization of the Buddha qualities in oneself; b) mindfulness of the purity that is emptiness is the realization of the emptiness of the deity and of all other phenomena.

3) Holding firmly to the diamond perfection of oneself as deity: we must stabilize this practice, sustaining it until we become one with the state of enlightenment. See also notes 60 and 62.

58. The three examples of illusion are: the body is like an image, the voice is like an echo, the mind is like the movement of a cloud in the sky.

The twelve examples of illusion are: illusory beings, the reflection of the moon in water, a shadow, a mirage, a dream body, an echo, the city of Gandharva, clouds and hallucinations, a rainbow, lightning, bubbles, an image.

59. "Ordinariness" refers to the everyday appearance of objects and one's assent to that appearance.

60. Attainment of the purity of the natural signs refers to attainment of the Form Body of a Buddha. Attainment of the purity of emptiness refers to attainment of the Truth Body of a Buddha. In order to attain Buddhahood, one must attain both these Bodies of a Buddha.

Attaining the Form Body requires completion of the accumulation of merit, and attainment of the Truth Body requires completion of the accumulation of wisdom. It is from this point of view that merit and wisdom are seen as the 'causes' of Buddhahood.

61. 'Fruit of separation' refers to 32 mental qualities of Buddha: 18 special qualities, 10 powers, and four fearlessnesses. 'Fruit of ripening' refers to the 32 major marks of a Buddha.

62. We need to stabilize in this deity yoga stage of generation: first oneself clearly visualized as a deity, then the realization of the pure state of emptiness and the lack of inherent existence. We must maintain that state until we become one with it; to do it once, for half an hour, and then forget it — that is not enough.

63. This means that the light radiates from your heart, filling all of space. The light touches all phenomena and sentient beings; thoroughly purified, these then dissolve back into your heart.

64. Guru yoga is both a preparatory practice (pages 34-38) and a main branch of the fivefold path (pages 58-71); one is simple, the other profound. The first is general guru yoga: devotion to one's teacher and seeing that teacher as Vajradhara. The second is the detailed guru yoga practice: actually to establish the four bodies of the Buddha.

In order to achieve the Buddha Bodies actually in oneself, one visualizes them and visualizes becoming one with them, to invoke their qualities. Invoking a quality brings enlightenment in that quality; each of the bodies must be cultivated. The practice of guru yoga with intense devotion is the only way to attain the completion stage — to attain the mahamudra state.

65. One's teacher is viewed as a Buddha; and the teacher's four bodies are viewed as the Four Bodies of a Buddha.

66. The prayer-mantra to the Emanation Body is given on page 63. The three conceptions are: of inherently existent agent, action, and object. See also note 24.

67. The crown-protrusion of the Buddha is said to be visible only to those of sufficient merit.

68. With regard to one's own practice, maintaining the ethic of vows involves cultivating virtuous states of mind during practice and working to eliminate mental obstacles to practice. In relation to the practice of others, this ethic is maintained by eliminating obstacles to their practice, providing them with facilities for practice, and so on.

69. The eight offerings of Samantabhadra are visualized as being made up of the good qualities of the deities. These eight offerings are: water offering, washing one's feet, offering flowers, incense, fire, scented water, food, and music.

70. While making the eight offerings: One maintains the ethics of accumulating virtue by imagining these offerings to be vast and limitless, made of infinite good qualities. One maintains the ethics for the sake of sentient beings by dedicating them to other sentient beings. One maintains the ethics of vows by visualizing that all afflictions (of oneself and others) are cleared away.

71. Each goddess becomes two, then three, and so on until

there are innumerable manifestations of each of the five types of offering goddesses.

72. The mind in the natural, nonartificial state is not simply "emptied"; it is at rest, without meditative effort. This is discussed on pages 85-88.

73. The visualization of this assembly was described on page 60. Around the outwardly established Emanation Body — the teacher-deity Shakyamuni — are Buddhas, Bodhisattvas, and offering goddesses. The dissolving into oneself completes the first meditation in guru yoga and leads into the second meditation, that of the Complete Enjoyment Body. Each stage leads into the next.

The sequence establishes the Emanation Body as activity (page 60), the Complete Enjoyment Body (Vairochana) as good qualities (page 63), the Truth Body (the Lama Vairochana) secretly as nonduality (page 68), and the Nature Body as suchness (page 70).

74. The prayer-mantra of the Kagyu lamas is given on pages 64-67.

75. All of the preceding visualization, as well as the dissolving into emptiness described here, is seen as happening at one's own heart.

76. This mantra is given on page 69.

77. The ten grounds are the ten Bodhisattva grounds or levels of attainment. Each of the two vehicles, Hinayana and Mahayana, contains five paths: of accumulation, preparation, seeing, meditation, and no-more-learning.

78. In the meditation on the Nature Body there is no visualization of a deity. Here we are concerned with realization of the basic mind.

79. This mind of meditative experience free of duality does not come without a lot of study and practice. Itself, it is not a practice, though the practices are necessary to its realization. When it is talked about, then duality enters into it.

In the relative, everything is there; in the absolute state is nothing, no thing. In the relative mind we have all these activities — but then we leave that state. Emptiness is not really a practice, it is the profound state of mahamudra; it is also a way of describing one quality of mind, the quality of being without thought. For a beginner, 'no thought' means an empty head, but that is not what is meant.

80. The three types of obstructions are: karmic obstructions, obstructions to liberation, and obstructions to omniscience. Generally, karmic obstructions are included within the category of obstructions to liberation.

81. 'The view is the unmistaken realization of the meaning (the true nature) of the mind' (page 91). The correct view of the true nature of phenomena (including the mind) is inseparable from the nonmistaken realization of that true nature by a nondual wisdom consciousness. The true nature of phenomena is emptiness — mahamudra.

82. Before students can establish the view, a teacher who has truly realized it must give instructions, 'this is the view'; it is like pointing out the moon. The disciples then understand that view and practice it, but they do not yet realize the view in the sense arising from meditation. It is a realization depending on instructions. For some students the view is very difficult to understand, so while the teacher is pointing, he or she uses a lot of reasoning and examples, and the students do a lot of analysis. But eventually the students are to see the moon themselves, the Buddha's qualities have to appear; and for that the disciples must meditate.

83. To settle the view means to understand the mode of abiding of phenomena; it involves analysis of the true nature of objects and of subjects.

84. The two stains of conceptuality are the obstructions to liberation and omniscience.

85. Because these reasonings are given in detail in the Madhyamika texts, Kunga Rinchen merely mentions them here. An elaboration of these reasonings can be found in *Emptiness Yoga*, by Jeffrey Hopkins (Ithaca, NY: Snow Lion Publications, 1986).

86. If one says to oneself 'all is emptiness,' this is not realization of emptiness; it is just thinking. This is the case in all four of these mistakes, the problem of not understanding the basis.

87. Literally: a 'meaning generality' (*arthasāmānya* in Sanskrit; *don spyi* in Tibetan) of emptiness.

88. When the basis is not understood, one may try to deal with afflictive emotions and suffering by pushing them out of one's mind and thinking about 'emptiness.' That is not correct. It is not understanding that the obstruction and the antidote are the same, that all phenomena are the nature of emptiness.

89. Inner phenomena are consciousnesses, sense powers, and so forth.

90. The three great views are Madhyamika, Mahamudra, and the view known as *Dzok-chen* in Tibetan.

91. Each of the three great views explains phenomena and emptiness a little differently and therefore involves some assertion; and where there is assertion there is duality. With the faults of duality, the view cannot be realized — that is, cannot be known unmistakenly and nonconceptually. The real view is without assertion. When one really realizes the true fact of the view of all phenomena, one can give it any name. In this system it is called mahamudra, but that is only a name, and the true nature is beyond all names. It simply is, as fire is hot, and there is nothing to accept or reject.

92. A person attached to high status is one who would take pride, for example, in being Madhyamika, or in being a mahamudra practitioner. If you are not free from such pride, you cannot realize the ultimate view, which is free of assertion. One who does realize the view free of assertion is said to be untouched by any view; that is, untouched by any dualistic assertion.

93. Beginning practitioners have formal practice sessions, but Kunga Rinchen is not now talking to them. The early practice is cultivated by ordinary study and attention, the real practice by aspiration and compassion. At first one can do only the first kind, then the second kind comes little by little. Eventually, illumination is spontaneous and continual, whether one is doing the formal practice or not.

It is the same with the dedication. You do the practice all the time and the dedication all the time. Dedication is not just something done at the end of a session; dedication means that whatever you do you dedicate to the attaining of enlightenment.

94. 'With signs' means with an object appearing to the mind. There is no analysis, but there is an object, the mustard seed at the heart. This meditation balances the mind and is a profound method for developing calm-abiding. When the mind is well balanced, one no longer needs to concentrate on an object; this is 'without signs.'

95. 'Natural state' means without effort; the mind rests quietly whether there is an object or not. See also pages 85-86.

96. The 'natural nonartificial state' is without effort and well

balanced. See also pages 85-86.

97. The four aspects of mindfulness are: stabilization of the body, stabilization of feeling, stabilization of the mind, stabilization of virtue. The four perfect abandonments are: abandoning the arising nonvirtues, not allowing to arise that which has not yet arisen, generating the antidote to nonvirtues, increasing the antidote that has been generated. The four foundations of miraculous power are: the meditative stabilization of aspiration, the meditative stabilization of joyous effort, the meditative stabilization of mindfulness, the meditative stabilization of analysis. The five powers are: power of faith, power of effort, power of mindfulness, power of concentration, power of wisdom. The five controlling powers are: controlling power of faith, controlling power of effort, controlling power of mindfulness, controlling power of concentration, controlling power of wisdom. The seven branches of enlightenment are: perfect mindfulness, perfect discriminating awareness, perfect perseverance, perfect joy, perfect taming of mind and body, perfect concentration, perfect equanimity. The noble eightfold path consists of: right view, right thought, right speech, right action, right livelihood, right effort, right mindfulness, right concentration.

98. The naked mind is the basic mind, or mahamudra; see discussion of the basic mind in the section on quintessential instructions, pages 89-93.

99. The true nature of one's mind cannot be described. The realization of that true nature is called mahamudra or 'the wisdom of self-awareness.' Such realization is without distinction of subject and object. Thus, mahamudra is both the true nature of the mind — its emptiness — and the basic mind itself.

100. Here, 'the meaning of the mind' refers to the true or ultimate nature of the mind. See note 81.

101. That appearance and mind 'abide as a self-liberating unity' means that appearance and mind are ultimately one; they are pure — beginninglessly free of impurity or obstruction.

102. 'Emptiness dawns as cause and effect' means emptiness is seen as that which makes cause and effect possible. Cause and effect are seen as the sport, or manifestation, of emptiness. It is because objects are empty (without inherent existence) that they can function as cause and effect. It is because they are empty of inherent existence that the perfect causes and conditions (the

collections of merit and wisdom) result in the perfect effect or fruit (Buddhahood).

103. Sustaining the practice of mahamudra takes place at the Mahayana path of meditation. Having attained direct perception of mahamudra on the path of seeing, one practices. One keeps on practicing over and over, developing it more and more, slowly uncovering all the qualities, the bodies, of the Buddha. The attaining of direct special insight realizing mahamudra is at the Mahayana path of seeing and is also the first of the ten Bodhisattva grounds (see note 77). The practice of mahamudra goes on until enlightenment is achieved: the path of no-more-learning. This is called cultivation of the Truth Body, the bringing out of it.

104. The *dakorma* dedication is named after the first three syllables of the prayer used in this dedication. The prayer is translated on page 100.

105. The Buddha nature, which is the pure absolute state, is called the root of virtue. The root of virtue in us is always there, but it is like a seed: if we don't plant it, it won't grow. Dedication is the planting. Or it is like a drop of water: if we let it fall on the ground it will vanish, but if we throw it into the ocean it will not dry until the ocean dries. So our drop of virtue can be destroyed by afflictive emotions if we don't dedicate it; but if we dedicate that drop to the ocean of wisdom, then — even if afflictive emotions come — it will remain in the ocean and help all sentient beings achieve enlightenment.

106. The innate virtue is the object we dedicate, and dedication without object is the way we do it. When we begin, we think 'I am here, these are what I dedicate, this is the being to whom I dedicate it' — all duality. But with understanding and practice, all of these become like the moon and its reflection — they are just visible but are not really existing, not really separate things. It depends on the person whether this is realized or not.

'Without object of observation' means without duality. There is visualization, and if the practitioner sees just his visualization or if he thinks 'this is true, that is not true,' then there is duality. But if he understands the visualization to be (as are all phenomena) like the moon's reflection, then there is no duality. That is why dedication without object of observation is called the unsurpassed dedication, beyond duality and nonduality.

It is sometimes said that if there is an object of observation there has to be duality and that only a Buddha can see the object and the emptiness at the same time. This is true, but the practitioner, though not a Buddha, is trying to practice the Buddha's wisdom quality. We try to have the kind of consciousness that can see the object and emptiness at the same time. Only a Buddha can do it — and only by trying can one become a Buddha.

107. Sphere of reality *(dharmadhātu):* see note 45.

108. To 'establish in Buddhahood' is also expressed on page 102 as to 'bring to fruition' and means to establish all sentient beings in the enlightened state. This is the dedication of the innate virtue.

109. The eight worldly concerns are: concern with gaining wealth and losing wealth, with pleasure and pain, with fame and disgrace, with kind words and harsh words.

The four causes of cyclic existence are: the contaminants of desire, existence (desire in the form and formless realms), ignorance, and wrong views.

110. Wisdom that is 'free of the three spheres' is free of the conceptions of inherently existent agent, action, and object (see note 24). Such wisdom is also said to be 'without object of observation.'

111. Buddhahood is called an ornament wheel because the infinite good qualities of that state are never-ending.

Index

abandonments, the four 83, n.97
Abhisamayālaṃkāra quoted 101
abiding, production, and cessation 71, 90; *see also* calm-abiding, mode of abiding
accomplishment, actual 31, 35, n.26; the highest 70; *see also siddhi* accumulation: of compassion and wisdom 34, n.13; of merit and wisdom 55, n.5, 60; of virtue 61, n.70; Mahayana path of n.77; *see also* collections
accumulations, the two 97
acceptance and rejection: the correct 94; action free from 93
action, object, and agent (the three conceptions) 62, 64, n.24, 66 actions: and effects 75; of body, speech, and mind cause suffering 91; and afflictions 99
activity 59, 60, 73; virtuous 91
afflictions 19, n.24; lama is victorious over 70; cloud is symbol of 72; to annihilate 88, are not different from Truth Body 92
aggregates 53; five, are the five Buddhas 54; are not inherently existent 93

aggregation, transitory, called I and mine 87
āḥ (syllable) 32, 34, 51, 52, 64, 68, 69
Akshobhya 52, 55
ambrosia 31
Amoghasiddhi 55
analysis: *see* reasoning
animals 28, n.40
antidotes 23, 76, n.11, 88
appearance 92; clear, of the deity 55; special and ordinary 56, n.59; is mind 74, 75; unity of emptiness and 92, n. 55
appearance and mind (object and subject) 92; are a unity 92, n.101
appearances: are the body of the deity 56; all objects are 73; mode of abiding of 73; to understand as Truth Body 94
Arhaṭ (Foe Destroyer) 100
artificial, nonartificial 85, 86; *see also* natural
ārūpyadhātu n.40
aspects, three of body, four of speech, three of mind 28
aspiration 94, 97, n.97
assembly 34; of Superiors (the san-

Printed in the United States
by Baker & Taylor Publisher Services